UNIFORM CIVIL CODE
TOWARDS UNIFIED BHARAT

PIYUSH GUPTA

Foreword by: Justice Adarsh Kumar Goel

Assisted by: Jai Saini & Isha Kapoor

BLUEROSE PUBLISHERS
India | U.K.

Copyright © Piyush Gupta 2023

All rights reserved by author. No part of this publication may be reproduced, stored in a retrieval system or transmitted in any form or by any means, electronic, mechanical, photocopying, recording or otherwise, without the prior permission of the author. Although every precaution has been taken to verify the accuracy of the information contained herein, the publisher assumes no responsibility for any errors or omissions. No liability is assumed for damages that may result from the use of information contained within.

BlueRose Publishers takes no responsibility for any damages, losses, or liabilities that may arise from the use or misuse of the information, products, or services provided in this publication.

For permissions requests or inquiries regarding this publication, please contact:

BLUEROSE PUBLISHERS
www.BlueRoseONE.com
info@bluerosepublishers.com
+91 8882 898 898
+4407342408967

ISBN: 978-93-93385-43-7

Cover design: Muskan Sachdeva
Typesetting: Pooja Sharma

First Edition: December 2023

Dedication

Dedicated to my pillar of strength, my loving grandfather, Late Sh. Dhan Prakash Gupta who was a great advocate, a renowned author of 24 books, and a philanthropist. I would have been nothing without his values & guidance.

Justice Adarsh Kumar Goel
Former Judge Supreme Court of India
Chairperson
National Green Tribunal

Faridkot House
Copernicus Marg
New Delhi-110001
Tel. : 011-23043507

06.07.2023

Foreword

This book presents valuable study material on hotly debated issue of Uniform Civil Code (UCC), which is Constitutional mandate under article 44. The author has compiled relevant material with reference to historical perspective, international practices, Constituent Assembly debates, earlier legislations, Law Commission report, Court judgements and public opinion. The Book also discusses how UCC is not against any religion and will pave way for justice, equality and unified Bharat consistent with the preambular objective of promoting fraternity amongst the citizens, leading to unity and integrity of the nation.

The author has duly acknowledged, in the endnotes of each chapter, books and articles on the subject which are the sources of the information compiled in the book.

As pointed out by the author, a Division Bench of Bombay High Court comprising the then Chief Justice Chagla and Justice Gajendragadkar in famous case of *State of Bombay Vs. Narsu Appa Mali*, AIR 1952 Bom 84, upheld the Prevention of Hindu Bigamous Marriages Act, 1946, prohibiting Bigamy in Hindus, modifying the Hindu religious practice to the contrary. It referred to US Supreme Court judgement authored by Justice Field in *Davis v. Beason*, (1889) 133 U. S. 637. The US Supreme Court held that marriage is a civil contract to be regulated by law. Such law does not violate freedom of religion in any manner. Thus, law to prohibit bigamous marriage was held to be measure of social reform for gender justice.

Supreme Court judgements inter alia in *Shah Bano* (1985), *Jordon* (1985), Sarla Mudgal (1995) and *Sayra Bano* (2017) categorically support need for UCC.

The book refers to practices in Muslim countries, modifying *Sharia* Law, showing that *Sharia* Law is not essential part of religion.

Residence : 7A, Motilal Nehru Marg, New Delhi-110 011
Phone : 011-2379 2255, 2301 6245

When UCC was put forth in Constituent Assembly, it was projected that such reform does not violate right to religion. Eminent Constituent Assembly members like K.M. Munshi and A.K. Ayyar supported UCC and Dr. Ambedkar included the same as Article 44 by stating that even Muslims may not be against it.

Author points out that when Hindu Code Bill was proposed, eminent parliamentarians of that time - N.C. Chatterjee and S.P. Mukherjee stated that reform should not be limited to Hindu society, excluding Muslims or other religions in the name of secularism. However, the then PM Nehru held the view that there being opposition by some Muslims, law reform should be confined to Hindus. View of Nehru is no longer supported by experience on the ground and has resulted in continuing injustice to Muslim women. The author has also relied on the views of eminent Muslim scholars like Dr. Tahir Mahmood. Law must march with changing social needs.

The author has thus found overwhelming view to canvas that far from diluting the principle of secularism, UCC will be a step towards national integration.

I hope the book will be of great interest and value to all its readers. I wish the book and the author great success.

(Adarsh Kumar Goel)

Justice M.C. Garg
Senior Advocate
(Former Judge - M.P. & Delhi High Court)

Dear Piyush,

It is with great pleasure that I extend my warmest congratulations to you on the publication of your remarkable book, ***Uniform Civil Code: Towards Unified Bharat.*** This exceptional work delves into the intricacies of personal laws in India, shedding light on the significance of a Uniform Civil Code (UCC) and its potential to foster harmony and equality among diverse communities.

In this thought-provoking book, you have skilfully navigated the complex terrain of personal laws that govern individuals based on their religious affiliations, caste, faith and beliefs. With meticulous attention to detail, the author elucidates the profound considerations underlying the creation of these laws, which are deeply rooted in customs and religious texts. Notably, your effort in emphasizing the differences between the personal laws of Hindus and Muslims, showcasing the foundations upon which they are built and Hindu personal law drew from ancient texts such as the Vedas, Smritis and Upanishads is appreciable.

The extensive research, insightful analysis and eloquent presentation in this significant contribution to the field of legal scholarship, will serve as a valuable resource for academics, policymakers, legal professionals and all those interested in fostering a more egalitarian society.

Mool Chand Garg

JUSTICE VINOD GOEL
FORMER JUDGE HIGH COURT OF DELHI

Dated: 14.07.2023

GOOD WISHES

It is with great pleasure that I extend my warmest congratulations to **Piyush Gupta** on the publication of his remarkable book, **Uniform Civil Code: Towards Unified Bharat.** This exceptional work delves into the intricacies of personal laws in India, shedding light on the significance of a Uniform Civil Code (UCC) and its potential to foster harmony and equality among diverse communities.

In this thought-provoking book, **Piyush Gupta** skillfully navigates the complex terrain of personal laws that govern individuals based on their religious affiliations, caste, faith, customs and beliefs. The author skillfully navigates the historical backdrop, offering readers a detailed exploration of India's rich history of multiculturalism and diversity. By examining the evolving society of India, the book illustrates how the need for a Uniform Civil Code has arisen as a result of the country's continuous social transformation. The author sheds light on the judiciary's unwavering support for the implementation of a UCC in accordance with Article 44 of the Constitution of our great country Bharat. By examining notable judicial decisions, the book highlights the judiciary's commitment to safeguarding individuals who face oppression and seeks to promote national cohesion and integrity.

I commend **Piyush Gupta** for his extensive research, insightful analysis, and eloquent presentation in this significant contribution to the field of legal scholarship. It is my belief that this book shall contribute significantly to the ongoing discourse and encourage informed discussions on the importance and implications of implementing a Uniform Civil Code in our country Bharat.

Best Wishes,

Justice Vinod Goel,
Former Judge, High Court of Delhi.

Office: B-10, Second Floor, Jangpura Extension
New Delhi-110014 M-9910384637
e-mail ID: justicevinodgoel@gmail.com

JUSTICE G.S. SISTANI
FORMER JUDGE DELHI HIGH COURT

It is with great pleasure that I extend my congratulations to **Piyush Gupta** on the publication of his book, **Uniform Civil Code: Towards Unified Bharat**. This exceptional work delves into the intricacies of personal laws in India, shedding light on the significance of a Uniform Civil Code (UCC) and its potential to foster harmony and equality among diverse communities.

In this thought-provoking book, **Piyush Gupta** skillfully navigates the complex terrain of personal laws that govern individuals based on their religious affiliations, caste, faith, and beliefs. With meticulous attention to detail, the author elucidates the profound considerations underlying the creation of these laws, which are deeply rooted in customs and religious texts. Notably, **Piyush Gupta** emphasizes the differences between the personal laws of Hindus and Muslims, showcasing the foundations upon which they are built. Hindu personal law drawn from ancient texts such as the Vedas, Smritis, and Upanishads, while simultaneously incorporating modern concepts of justice, equality, and conscience.

I commend **Piyush Gupta** for his extensive research, insightful analysis, and eloquent presentation in this significant contribution to the field of legal scholarship. It is my belief the book will serve as a valuable resource for academics, policymakers, legal professionals, and all those interested in fostering a more egalitarian society.

With warm regards,

G.S. Sistani

TALWANT SINGH
Advocate Supreme Court
Former Judge, Delhi High Court

X-19 (GF), Hauz Khas
New Delhi – 110016
Ph: 011- 41759309

Dear Piyush Ji,

I humbly express my deepest gratitude for your gracious consideration in selecting me to partake in the esteemed task of reviewing your illustrious book.

Beginning with the title itself, which is "Uniform Civil Code: Towards Unified Bharat" is an absolute fit for the book which talks about the problems India faced before its Constitution was framed, and the challenges that still exist today regarding Uniform Civil Code in India. It also compares India with other countries, showing how customs, cultures, and religions affect Indian society. The book focuses on the need for a Uniform Civil Code, which means having the same set of laws for everyone in the country. It explains why having such a code can help create a fair and inclusive society.

The book also addresses the misconceptions and debates surrounding this topic, trying to provide clear explanations. It talks about the different personal laws that different communities follow and how they impact individuals. The book also looks at how other countries deal with uniform civil codes, giving readers a better understanding of the issue.

There have been discussions in India about implementing a Uniform Civil Code, but there are concerns about how it might affect minority communities and the country's diverse society. This topic is important and controversial, so it is crucial to present one's ideas in a clear and understandable way and hence, I congratulate you for being able to achieve this goal.

Implementing a Uniform Civil Code is a subject that sparks passionate debate because it has different implications for different people. It is important to understand that there are various perspectives to this issue. One should approach it with respect and fairness as one explores its complexities. As a writer, it is essential to connect with readers and understand their thoughts. I appreciate the opportunity to contribute to this important discussion and share ideas with others.

Once again, I am grateful to you for considering me to contribute my thoughts to this important topic, and wishing you all the very best in your journey of publishing this book.

Thanks,

Justice Talwant Singh (Retd.)
Delhi High Court
Dated: 22.07.2023

Mobile: +91 99103 84653　　　　Email: talwant@nasdeep.in　　　　Web: nasdeep.in

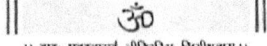

|| ॐ ||
|| वादः प्रवदतामाहं नीतिरस्मि जिगीषताम् ||

Alok Kumar
Advocate
Working President - Vishva Hindu Parishad
Patron - Dadhichi Deh Dan Samiti
Ex. Dy. Speaker - Delhi Vidhan Sabha

MESSAGE

The Constitution of India directs the Government's, both at the Centre and the States to endeavour, enact Uniform Civil Code for_all citizens of India throughout the territory of Bharat.

All members of parliament and of state assemblies enter the parliament or the assembly after taking oath of 'true faith and allegiance' to the Constitution of India.

But yet, in 73 years of Indian Constitution the Uniform Civil Code has not been enacted.

The Supreme Court of India in Sarla Mudgal and other cases have repeatedly emphasized the necessity of urgently enacting the UCC.

It is a matter of satisfaction that on the reference of Government of India the Law Commission of India (LCI) has begun consultations on the Uniform Civil Code.

This matter requires a mature and in-depth understanding. I am so happy that Shri Piyush Gupta Advocate has authored a book on this subject. Piyush Ji has provided an insightful understanding of all aspects of UCC and has put them in a easy flowing way to understand.

I believe that this book has come at very opportune moment and shall be widely used.

My best wishes.

आलोक कुमार

Alok Kumar, Senior Advocate

K.K. MANAN
ADVOCATE
CHAIRMAN

BAR COUNCIL OF DELHI
Head Off. : 2/6, Siri Fort Instutional Area,
Khel Gaon Marg, New Delhi - 110 049
Phone : 26498356, 26495195, 26495196
Branch Office : 1-F, Lawyers' Chambers,
High Court of Delhi, New Delhi - 110 003
Phone : 23387701

Ref. No. ....

Dated 18.07.2023

Dear Piyush Gupta,

I hope this letter finds you in the best of health and spirits. I am writing to you today to express my heartfelt appreciation and admiration for your exceptional work on the book "Uniform Civil Code: Towards Unified Bharat." Having recently immersed myself in the thought-provoking pages of your book, I felt compelled to convey my sincere gratitude and share my thoughts on this extraordinary literary endeavour.

I was deeply impressed by the comprehensive nature of your work, as you navigated the diverse historical, cultural, and religious aspects that have shaped India's legal framework. Furthermore, I commend you on your thoughtful and inclusive approach throughout the book.

In closing, I want to express my gratitude for your dedication and passion in delivering this invaluable literary piece to society. Your efforts have undoubtedly made a positive impact on the way we perceive the significance of a Uniform Civil Code, and I am certain that your book will continue to influence and inspire generations to come.

With my warmest wishes for your continued success and future endeavours.

Sincerely,

K K Manan, Sr. Advocate
Chairman, Bar Council of Delhi.

Contents

Chapter 1: Introduction 1

Chapter 2: The Authentic Foundation of Uniform Civil Code 16

Chapter 3: Judicial Pronouncements on Uniform Civil Code 54

Chapter 4: International Perspective Concerning UCC 79

Chapter 5: Law Commission Recommendations on the Uniform Civil Code 108

Chapter 6: UCC Is Not An Anti-Thesis To Religion 124

Chapter 7: Paving a Better Future for India 155

Chapter 8: From The Lens of Indian Women . 191

Chapter 9: The Wise Are With the UCC 218

Chapter 10: The Way Forward 237

About The Author 263

CHAPTER 1

Introduction

With the enactment of the Constitution of India in 1950, we as the citizens of the newly independent and diverse nation, gave ourselves a unified set of provisions which entails the ambition of a newly founded nation along with the ideals which were to be adhered solemnly as we soar to the new heights as a nation. As the days wore on, standardized set of rules and procedures were adopted with the idea of fostering Uniform laws to promote consistency and efficiency in the legal system.

To mould this vision of having uniformity in personal laws into reality, the makers of the constitution included article 44 (among other implicit articles) as an obligation upon the state to endeavour to secure for citizens a uniform civil code. The Uniform Civil Code (UCC) is a proposed legal framework that aims to replace personal laws based on religious practices with a common set of civil laws applicable to all citizens of India. The implementation of a UCC has been a contentious issue in the country, with proponents arguing for its necessity to promote equality and secularism, while opponents cite concerns about cultural and religious diversity. The article was inserted as a reminder to effect integration of India by bringing various communities on the common platform on matters that are presently governed by diverse personal laws. The argument for a uniform civil code (UCC) is irrefutable in a modern nation state as long as it is rational, non-discriminatory and promotes social equality and gender justice. Multiple legal codes flout the principle of equality before the law. India's legal system is a complex web of overlapping laws and regulations. Implementing a UCC would require a comprehensive overhaul of existing personal laws, which can be a daunting task. Harmonizing diverse religious and cultural practices into a single code poses significant challenges, as it necessitates balancing the rights and interests of various communities

However, despite having a clear constitutional mandate on the issue whenever the demand for introducing Uniform Civil Code (hereinafter referred to as 'UCC') arises, various sections of society seem to be at loggerheads over its enactment and implementation. This book is a compilation of all the multi-faceted debates over the issue of enactment and implementation of UCC in the Indian democratic setup.

The chapter titled 'The Authentic Foundation of Uniform Civil Code' talks about the legislative history of the aforementioned issue. Further, the chapter is bifurcated into two parts, where one-part sheds light on the pre-constitutional views on the issue of UCC and the second part elucidates the developments after the introduction of the constitution of India. In furtherance of the aforementioned discussion, the development in various statutes dealing with the personal laws of the citizens has also been evaluated. To lay down the groundwork for the upcoming discussions, the arguments put forth during Constitutional assembly debates, Bills laid down in either house of the parliament as well as the works of the key contributors who have got the progression of the UCC as a subject matter to the level on which it stands today. Based on the deliberations put forth, the Chapter further enlarges the discussion by identifying the key figures in the discussion and how they played a major role in the furtherance of this idea of having a Uniform Civil Code. The authentic foundation of a Uniform Civil Code in India lies in its potential to foster social justice, gender equality, and national integration. While the path to its implementation may be challenging, creating a legal framework that ensures equal rights and opportunities for all citizens is imperative. A well-crafted Uniform Civil Code can reinforce the principles of secularism and contribute to a more harmonious and inclusive society in India.

The chapter titled as *'Judicial Pronouncement on Uniform Civil Code'* provides the views that have been put forward by the judiciary from time to time on the discussion pertaining to UCC. The Chapter includes various landmark judgments on the aforementioned matter, along with pertinent discussion pointing towards the essentiality of the implementation of a Uniform Civil Code. The desirability of the code has been stated time and again by various authorities including the apex and other High courts. There is a catena of judgements in which the courts have minced no meat in putting forwards the dire need for the implementation of UCC in the country. This chapter also includes the recent orders of the Hon'ble courts, whereby the judiciary has highlighted the role of the legislature in the implementation of the Uniform Civil Code.

The concept of a Uniform Civil Code (UCC) is not unique to India and has been a subject of discussion and implementation in various countries around the world. While the specifics and extent of UCC may differ across jurisdictions, the international perspective provides insights into different approaches and experiences regarding the implementation of a uniform civil code. The international perspective offers useful insights into various approaches and experiences, providing crucial insight for nations considering the adoption or revision of their civil laws. It is crucial to highlight that based on the unique legal, cultural, and historical circumstances of each nation, the application and scope of the Uniform Civil Code might vary considerably. The experiences of different nations highlight the potential benefits of a uniform legal framework, such as promoting equality, social cohesion, and gender justice. However, it is equally crucial to consider the sensitivities, religious diversity, and cultural nuances of a particular country along with numerous other social factors when formulating and implementing a Uniform code. The chapter titled *'International perspective with respect to UCC,* presents a holistic point of view with respect to the countries where similar code is either in force or has been implemented. What are all the counties where such laws have been introduced, or an attempt is being made to introduce such laws; how is the reception where such laws have already been introduced or their net effect on the legal system of the concerned nations; whether a success or a failure? These are a few questions, in the backdrop of which this chapter will proceed. The chapter begins by describing one of the earliest legal systems i.e., the Roman legal system. Afterwards, the chapter proceeds to explain the uniform civil laws of France, the unification movements in the USA, Uniform Child custody jurisdiction and Enforcement Act, Uniform Child Abduction Prevention Act etc. Along with these major statutes, landmark judicial pronouncements of these contemporary jurisdictions have also been mentioned for a better understanding of the topic. Position in Canada, Australia, Africa and the Middle East has also been discussed.

Observing the importance of a Uniform Civil Code, the Supreme Court in its landmark judgment of Shah Bano propounded that, "*A common Civil Code will help the cause of national integration by removing disparate loyalties to laws which have conflicting ideologies.*" Since Indian Judiciary has not taken a definite view on UCC, the issue remains a subject of political and societal debate in India. However, the Apex Court has observed in several cases that the implementation of the UCC would promote gender justice, equality, and secularism in the country. Overall, the chapter concludes with how the judiciary has stressed the importance of a uniform code in ensuring equality and justice to all citizens irrespective of religion, but the decision to implement it remains with the legislature and the executive.

The Law Commission of India plays a crucial role in shaping and reforming the legal system of the country. Established as a non-statutory body in 1955, its primary function is to examine and review existing laws, propose legal reforms, and recommend necessary changes to the government. The chapter titled as *'Law Commission Recommendations on the Uniform Civil Code'* elucidate and dissects the reports provided by the Law Commission on the subject matter of UCC. The chapter discusses in detail the Law Commission of India's report on "Reforms in the Hindu Marriage Act, 1955" (Report No. 252), the Commission recommended that the government take steps towards the implementation of a UCC. The discussion of the chapter in a nutshell would be that the Law Commission has argued that the implementation of a UCC would promote gender justice and equality, and would also bring greater clarity and consistency to the legal system. However, the Commission has acknowledged that implementing such a code would be a complex task and would require careful consideration of various religious and cultural sensitivities. The chapter is bifurcated into various sub-dimensions of the ongoing discussion. Initially, it examines the consultation paper and then further proceeds to discuss the recommendations of the consultation paper.

Religion plays a significant role in personal laws in India, and different religions have their own set of laws governing these matters. UCC has been a contentious issue in India for several decades, with some arguing that it is necessary for the country's secularism and to ensure gender justice and equality, while others argue that it is a threat to religious freedom and diversity. Some religious groups in India have opposed the implementation of the UCC, arguing that it would interfere with their religious practices and customs. However, others argue that the UCC would promote gender equality and justice, as it would ensure that all citizens, regardless of their religion, are governed by the same laws. In this pretext, the chapter titled *'Uniform Civil Code and Religion in India'* is perhaps one of the most significant ones in the book. The chapter begins by explaining the religious demography of India, simultaneously tracing the major religions, their distribution, and their historical and cultural significance. Moving further, the chapter discusses personal laws in India and various statutes governing the same. Towards the end, the chapter concludes by providing a viable solution for religious discord and how UCC can act as an effective tool to resolve religious discord in India by promoting a sense of equality and justice among all citizens, regardless of their religion.

The chapter titled *'Uniform Civil Code: Paving a better future for India'* talks about how UCC is advantageous for promoting a nationalistic spirit through uniformity. Further, the chapter enunciates how in a pluralistic society like India, people have faith in their religious beliefs or doctrines, making it challenging to implement Uniform Civil Code. The chapter sheds light on the issues of National integration, intergroup religious equality and simplification of laws. The existence of different personal laws based on religious practices and customs often leads to confusion and conflict, especially in cases involving inter-faith marriages and succession. A uniform civil code would help in resolving such conflicts by providing a clear legal framework for resolution. One of the main arguments in favour of a UCC is that it would ensure gender equality by providing a common set of laws applicable to all citizens, regardless of their religious affiliation. Indian women often face discrimination in personal matters governed by religious laws, such as marriage, divorce, and inheritance. Many women support the idea of a UCC as they believe it would guarantee equal rights and treatment in these areas. The existence of multiple personal laws based on religion creates confusion and complexity, particularly for women who are unaware of their rights or lack access to legal resources. A UCC would simplify the legal framework, making it more accessible and understandable for women. This would enable them to navigate legal processes more effectively and assert their rights with greater confidence. While many women advocate for a UCC, there are concerns about striking a balance between cultural identities and individual rights. It is important to ensure that the implementation of a UCC does not lead to the erasure of cultural diversity or the imposition of practices that are alien to certain communities. Women hope that a UCC would respect their cultural identities while also guaranteeing their fundamental rights. The chapter revolves around the thought that UCC would help in fostering national unity and integration by providing a common legal framework for all citizens of the country. To buttress the arguments, the views of several legal luminaries have also been referred to in this chapter. Various benefits of implementation such as the promotion of gender equality, ensuring social justice and simplification of legal procedures have also been discussed.

The chapter titled as '*Looking at UCC from the eyes of the Indian women*' vividly discusses the issues that women are facing due to the tyranny of personal laws. Personal laws discriminate against women in matters of marriage, divorce, custody of children, inheritance, and property rights. In addition to it, they are not given equal rights in matters of inheritance and property. The implementation of a Uniform Civil Code (UCC) in India has been a topic of discussion for many years. While proponents argue that a UCC would promote gender equality and women's rights, it is essential to examine the potential impact of such a code from the perspective of Indian women. This essay aims to explore the views and concerns of Indian women regarding the Uniform Civil Code. The present chapter seeks to look at the implementation of the Uniform Civil Code in India through the lens of women. The chapter also discusses how personal laws in India have long been skewed in favour of men, perpetuating discrimination against women in matters such as marriage, adoption, maintenance, and succession.

The chapter provides a vantage point with respect to a woman's perspective. It put forth the contentions of women as a category, on the issue of the Uniform code. The issue of gender justice in personal laws has been a contentious topic and has been cited as a reason to implement Uniform Civil Code, particularly after several Supreme Court decisions on the matter. The chapter ends with the conclusion that the Uniform Civil Code is particularly necessary because it will grant women in India equal rights, particularly because religion-based personal laws are misogynistic. From the perspective of Indian women, the implementation of a Uniform Civil Code holds the potential to address gender inequality, promote secularism, and protect women from discriminatory practices. They believe that a UCC would offer them equal rights, freedom of choice, and a simplified legal framework. However, it is crucial to approach the implementation of a UCC with sensitivity to cultural diversity, ensuring that women's rights are upheld without undermining their cultural identities. Engaging in inclusive dialogues and considering the perspectives and experiences of women from different backgrounds is crucial to shaping a UCC that truly advances gender equality in India. For its implementation, both religious and personal laws should be evaluated, and the best elements from all major religions as well as from other nations' personal laws should be gathered and used.

The chapter titled as *'The wise are with the UCC'* is a compilation of various prominent voices which have been echoing in favour of the implementation of the uniform code. The chapter beautifully weaves different opinions of doyens of law and other prominent figures and presents a holistic view regarding the essentiality of implementation of the UCC. This concept has received a myriad of responses and still continues to spark debates. The personal laws enacted by the colonial rulers have proved to be inconsistent and discriminatory from time to time. The issues regarding parity in inheritance rights for women, guardianship, interfaith marriages, and variation in the rights offered by these personal laws to different genders, are seldom discussed in depth. Intellectuals and progressive thinkers often support the implementation of a UCC as they see it as a means to promote social justice, secularism, and individual freedoms. They believe that a uniform set of laws applicable to all citizens, irrespective of their religious affiliations, would foster national integration, reduce social divisions, and uphold the principles of equality and secularism. Many legal experts and scholars argue in favour of a UCC, highlighting the need for a simplified and coherent legal framework. They point out that the existence of multiple personal laws based on religious practices creates complexity and confusion, leading to legal disputes and hindrances in access to justice. They believe that a UCC would streamline the legal system, enhance clarity, and ensure equal treatment under the law. Some political parties in India, particularly those with a secular and progressive ideology, support the implementation of a UCC. They view it as a step towards harmonizing diverse religious practices with the principles of equality and secularism. These parties often emphasize the importance of individual rights and freedoms and advocate for a unified legal framework that respects religious diversity while ensuring equal rights for all citizens. Social reformers and human rights organizations often endorse the idea of a UCC as it aligns with their objectives of promoting social equality, justice, and human rights. They argue that a UCC would address historical injustices, eliminate regressive practices, and pave the way for a more inclusive and progressive society.

It is worth noting that while there is support for a UCC, there are also dissenting voices and concerns raised by religious and cultural groups who fear the erosion of their identities and traditions. Achieving a consensus and addressing these concerns would be crucial in the formulation and implementation of a Uniform Civil Code in India.

India being a diverse nation, always have diverse opinion from different religions and communities and the application of the Uniform Civil Code will invite difference of opinion. This chapter also takes into account various bills proposed in either house of the parliament, various representations made to the ruling government and other significant statements made by the political leaders.

This book, owing to its rich and diverse inclusion of various views on the topic, can also act as a wonderful guide for one to start diving into the complex legal and social landscape of India as a democratic nation and its journey for the unification of personal laws. The book provides a vantage view to the topic of the Uniform Civil Code as it includes all the possible discussions around the topic along with the issues which are intertwined with the topic of the Uniform Civil Code with respect to the Indian democratic and social fabric.

CHAPTER 2

The Authentic Foundation of Uniform Civil Code

Personal laws are those that govern people based on their religion, caste, faith, and beliefs. These laws are made after due consideration of customs and religious texts. These laws distinctly mention the rules pertaining to marriage, divorce, maintenance, adoption, co-parenting, inheritance, succession, the partition of family property, guardianship, wills, gifts, charitable donations, etc. The personal laws of both Hindus and Muslims are based on their religious texts and scriptures. Hindu personal law is based on ancient texts like Vedas, Smritis, and Upanishads and modern concepts of justice, equality, conscience etc.

A. Legislative History

The Uniform Civil Code has been in discussions for a very long time. When spoken in the Indian context, the main aim of this Code would be to ensure that vulnerable communities which include women, children and religious minorities are protected along with fostering an atmosphere of nationalist unity [1]. It is envisioned that when the Code comes into play, all the religion-based laws such as Hindu Code Bill, and Sharia Laws, inter alia will be simplified to a great extent, as there will be much more uniformity in the entire nation. There are multiple aspects which would be covered under this code, and that would include marriage, divorce, inheritance, adoptions, and maintenance which would be made uniform in nature and every citizen of the country will be subject to the same law, keeping aside their religion and what they affiliate with [2].

Pre-Constitution Era

The legislative history of the Uniform Civil Code goes long back. In the British colonial era, the British government submitted a report in 1835 which stated and emphasized that there was an emergent need for uniformity in codifying the laws, with respect to contracts, evidence, crimes, inter alia, and it was further suggested that personal laws concerning individual religions should not be included within this codification [3]. This was the very first instance that the subject matter of the Uniform Civil Code came up and became a much-discussed topic thereafter. In October 1840, the infamous Lex Loci report came out which discussed the importance of having the Indian law codified, however, the exclusion of personal laws was still made a point in the report as well [4]. Finally, in 1859, after the Queen's proclamation, a complete non-interference in personal law was decided upon and therefore, the other laws were codified throughout the country, but the religious personal laws continued to operate as they were by their separate codes with applicability on different communities [5]. It is noteworthy that the personal laws were kept out of the codification process, which ultimately led to the debate on Uniform Civil Code getting bigger and throwing more light upon it. Had the codification procedure been inclusive of all laws since the very beginning, there would have been multiple hardships which would have been avoided. However, it would be wrong to state that a unified code would be an easy solution to all problems since it has its own set of demerits that it carries.

Constitutional Era

After the British colonization in India had come to an end, the legislative discussions about the Uniform Civil Code did not end. In 1941, B.N. Rau Committee was created in order to codify Hindu law as there was a drastic increase in the number of legislations which were all related to personal laws, and it was the responsibility of the Hindu Law

Committee to establish one single civil code to ensure that there was uniformity in these laws [6]. The Committee held multiple discussions and deliberated upon a lot of issues and gave their recommendations which were based on old scriptures, intending to provide and ensure that women have equal rights under the codified Hindu law [7]. Various acts were reviewed, and the committee concluded that suggested establishing a civil code which deals with Hindu marriage, divorce, and succession [8]. In parallel, when the drafting of the Constitution of India was taking place, multiple leaders including Jawaharlal Nehru and Dr B.R. Ambedkar pushed on the proposition that a Uniform Civil Code should be in place and therefore, within the Constitution the idea of a Uniform Civil Code was incorporated as a part of the Directive Principles of State Policy (DPSP) under Article 44 [9]. This move of incorporating the idea of the Uniform Civil Code under the DPSPs was because of the heavy debates that were taking place against the enforcement of the same as a codified law and the lack of knowledge as well as awareness among individuals, which exists till date and is a problem which needs to be catered to in a proper manner. However, pertaining to the Hindu Code, there were certain legislative reforms that took place during this period which were:

1. The Hindu Succession Act, of 1956 was passed so as to regulate the law governing both intestate and succession without a will within the Hindu, Jain, Sikh, and Buddhist communities [10]. This Act also made updates within the Hindu law of property and ensured affirmative changes in the domain of property rights and ownership amongst women and the inheritance that they would receive after the death of the father, however, this act was further amended in 2005 and more descendants were added to Class I heirs making it more comprehensive and it was ensured that the share of daughters would be equal to that of sons and what they receive [11]. A huge amount of disparity that was existing within the system was also reduced which was a very positive change to be noticed. The rights of daughters and women overall were recognized with the passage of time and as a result of the codification of these laws, an equal position was created in law, which is mandated as per the Constitution as well.

2. A very unique legislation called the Special Marriage Act was enacted in 1954 which provided for all the laws and regulations with regard to civil marriages and when any marriage takes place between two individuals from different religious orientations [12]. This

law was also a huge milestone that was achieved as before the enactment of this legislation, there was no personal law which regulated inter-religion marriages and with the help of this Act, many problems in that arena were eased out and a proper procedure was in place.

3. Lastly, many other legislations like the Hindu Marriage Act, the Minority and Guardianship Act, and the Adoptions and Maintenance Act also came into being [13]. The importance of these acts was realized, and many areas started being governed under the ambit of these.

While talking about the legislative history of the Uniform Civil Code, it is pertinent to note the judicial precedents which led to the development of its history and contributed largely towards it. In 1985, the Shah Bano Case took place, after which the discussions around the Uniform Civil Code erupted once again with more vigor and it was suggested that the Code be introduced to maintain uniformity, however, that could never happen as it was not introduced in the parliament [14]. The Supreme Court in this case and its judgement pronounced that, under the maintenance of wives, children and parent's provisions which comes under Section 125 of the Criminal Procedure Code, all citizens were included regardless of their religion and a recommendation to set up a Uniform Civil Code was also emphasized on by the court [15]. As a result of this happening, there were various movements, debates, and meetings that were held across the nation because this was an issue of utmost importance at that point in time. As a result of all these discussions, meetings and the historic judgement passed by the Supreme Court, the government passed the Muslim Women's (Right to Protection on Divorce) Act in 1986 which made Section 125 of the Criminal Procedure Code inapplicable to Muslim women [16]. It can be stated herein that as a result of this act being passed in the first place, the sanctity of personal laws of each religion being applicable only to that religion was maintained but the efforts to have a uniform law that would apply to every individual failed once again as section of Muslim women were excluded from the coverage of the Criminal Procedure Code.

The Muslim Women's Act was challenged in the Daniel Latifi case, on the ground that it violated the fundamental rights of an individual covered under the same, which then led to the Supreme Court harmonizing the Act with Section 125 of the Criminal Procedure Code, to maintain the fact that no woman should be deprived of her right to receive maintenance and should not suffer because of that reason in the absence of provisions supporting the same [17]. This case was a huge win not only for the section of aggrieved Muslim women who were at the receiving end of the atrocities because the law not supporting them but for the entire nation because a precedent was set in a manner such that no one can take advantage of the law and escape without providing maintenance which is a right.

Therefore, it can be stated with surety that the legislative history of the Uniform Civil Code can be traced way back and there are deliberations that continue to take place to make it a reality but nothing concrete has come up in that regard as of now as it continues to be a part of the Constitution as a Directive Principle of State Policy.

B. Constituent Assembly Debates

A deeper insight into the history of the Uniform Civil Code can be gauged after a good reading of the Constituent Assembly Debates, which help in providing the background as to how in today's date the Code is treated and its stature. After India got independent, the debate around personal laws kept continuing and many deliberations happened over the same. In front of the Constituent Assembly, the issue was constantly discussed and debated by various legislators who had polarizing views on the subject matter. These Constituent Assembly Debates happened during the framing of the Constitution and in that process, many facts came into the picture concerning the utility of the Uniform Civil Code and what relevance it holds along with what should be its ultimate fate in the Constitution. Multiple Muslim members were of the view that this Code should not be enacted across India as it would have an impact on the idea of a 'secular state', and to support this they put forth their views on the evaluation of the Uniform Civil Code and how it should be treated and its applicability [18]. The first meeting of the Constituent Assembly took place in December 1946 wherein the framers of the Constitution decided and visioned that India would be a sovereign, democratic republic nation which would be founded on the ideas of liberty, justice, fraternity, and equality [19]. It is pertinent to note that the terms secularism and socialism were incorporated later into the Preamble in 1976 so as to support the right to freedom of religion which was present in the Constitution before [20]. Therefore, because of this, the constant debate around personal laws kept on continuing and even before in the Constituent Assembly this issue was discussed a great deal. In the November 1948 session, the topic of the Uniform Civil Code was elaborately discussed in the Constituent Assembly [21].

The discussion was initiated by Mahboob Ali Baig wherein he stated that there is an existing notion concerning what exactly a 'secular state' should be and that it is necessary that such a state should have common law present for its citizens for all aspects like culture, language, day-to-day lives, inter alia, however, this is not the correct way to look at it because of the very fact that in a secular state, there are citizens of different religious backgrounds who live together and they must have the freedom to practice their own religion and observe the laws that are applicable to them [22]. He lastly stated that, in his opinion, a civil code should not cover the personal laws of individuals of any state and such an interpretation should be followed by the framers as well when they are drafting the Constitution and including the idea of a Civil Code within the same [23].

Thereafter, Mr B. Pocker Sahib Bahadur stood up and supported this motion and, in his arguments, stated that he aligns with the argument presented by Mohamed Ismail as well, wherein he had suggested that a proviso should be added to Article 35 of the Constitution to ensure that no person, group or community shall be obliged to give up their personal laws [24]. Arguing and supporting his stance further, he mentioned that, it would be reasonable to amend Article 35 not only from the viewpoint of the Muslim community but all the other communities as well who follow different codes of law with regard to various matters like marriage, inheritance, adoptions, inter alia; furthermore, the freedom that India has achieved as a country should also include the freedom of conscience and religious practices which include following one's own religious laws rather than imposing one common code throughout the nation [25]. It is extremely pertinent to note here that the members of the Muslim community are not against the enactment of the civil code in its entirety, but they only have reservations when it comes to the inclusion of personal laws within the ambit of this code. This is clarified when Mr B. Pocker Bahadur argued the intention behind the Uniform Civil Code and whether it only applies to procedural matters and if it does, there would hardly be any objection from any community to implement the same, however, when it comes to matters involving marriage, inheritance, endowments, etc., it should be established that the personal laws shall be maintained and not be tampered with because even the members present in the Assembly would not appreciate the fact that their laws are being made uniform and that the essence of Article 19 gets completely lost in the presence of such a code in the country [26]. He lastly submitted an appeal to close his argument and stated that the Uniform Civil Code should only be maintained as a directive principle of state policy under the Constitution.

In support of these arguments presented, Mr Hussain Imam gave his supporting views wherein he stated that India has an extremely diverse population with multiple cultures and religions existing in one place and to mark everyone with a single stamp would not only be impossible but will also not be in the interest of justice [27]. He presented several arguments in support of his stand which are noteworthy ranging from the fact that in a country where the weather is so different in every state to the education system, there cannot be a unified code, along with the fact that in the presence of multiple legislative bodies which are meant to legislate as per the requirements of their own people, the possibility of uniformity gets even further diluted [28]. Leaning on the plight of the backward classes, he argued that the manner of safeguarding the property of backward classes is different from others like in the Jharkhand region special protection has been given to the aboriginal population and there is a demand for the law to be diverse as well because of the communal differences which exist and the difference in intelligence and resources of the population [29]. If a comparison is made between the tribes of Assam with the population of Bombay, then multiple differences can be identified not only with regard to their economic conditions but also the struggles that each section has to face [30]. He lastly concluded his arguments by stating that a secular state does not mean an anti-religious state in fact, it refers to a state wherein the state is embracing all cultures with an equal amount of respect for their differences therefore, in order to maintain this within India, the uniform civil code as an idea should not be implemented.

In the interim of all these debates and arguments taking place, Mr M.A. Ayyangar intervened and stated that the Indian concept of a secular state basically translates to all religions existing equally with dignity and honour and therefore all the different communities should be allowed their own religion, and culture along with observing their own personal laws [31].

However, it is interesting to note that in opposition to what was stated by the Muslim members of the Constituent Assembly, the Hindu members had a completely different view and in their arguments that they put forth before the assembly this was reflected very clearly. K.M. Munshi stood up in the assembly and put forth his view on the Uniform Civil Code and stated that even if Article 35 of the Constitution was missing it would be in the interest of the parliament to form a Uniform Civil Code because the power of guaranteeing religious freedom which is vested with the parliament also allows them to regulate the activities with regard to religion [32]. He further mentioned and gave examples stating that in various Muslim countries like Egypt and Turkey, the personal laws of religious minorities were not protected and in some Muslim communities there was an absence of acceptance of the Sharia Law, further, personal laws essentially discriminate between persons on the basis of sex which is not permissible under the Constitution of India [33]. He concluded his arguments by stating that the Hindu Code does not confirm its provisions only to the Hindu minorities but is wide enough for other communities to be included within its ambit and that with the help of one civil code being in place, there would be lesser disputes which concern themselves, particularly with personal laws and those will be eradicated slowly [34].

The arguments presented by K.M. Munshi in the Constituent Assembly were supported by another Hindu member of the Assembly Mr A.K. Ayyar who went ahead to state that he agrees with all the arguments presented by Mr Munshi and that, a civil code will run in all departments of civil relation starting from the law of contracts to the law relating to marriage, succession, property and others and therefore, logically there should not be any objections to it, on a general principle [35]. He countered the previous arguments presented by the other members and stated that Uniform Civil Code aims to bring unity and not destroy it as there would be a common measure of agreement in all these matters [36]. Lastly, he concluded his remarks by stating that the Hindu code derives itself from various laws and is not self-contained and that a democratic nation should be run by one codified law which was not the case under the British Raj, therefore, the Uniform Civil Code should be brought into action and be implemented by the Assembly [37]

The most poignant remarks at the end of the debate were made by Honorable Dr B.R. Ambedkar wherein he was not in favour of the amendments and defended the right of the state to interfere in the personal laws of the communities, he went ahead and defended the fact that the applicable laws of different communities apply at the time being; further, in support of the Hindu as well as the Muslim members he explained the fact that the proposal was creating only power and not an obligation and therefore, the Muslim members should not get too engrossed in reading into Article 44 [38]. Moving on, Dr Ambedkar also stated that, even if on any given day such a Code were to be implemented then it would only apply to those who would consent to be a party to it and be governed by it and it would not be implemented in any manner which is forceful as that would violate the freedom of religion under Article 19 which is a fundamental right of citizens [39].

After all these elaborate debates had ended, Article 35 was accepted as a part of the Constitution and it can be stated that even though the Constitution empowers the enactment of a Uniform Civil Code, there is an essential element of seeking consent present in the same which is of utmost importance and should be discussed more often when the question of Uniform Civil Code and its applicability arises time and again. It has been observed that even decades after the Constitution has been framed and come into being, there are still multiple negotiations and debates ongoing in various parts of the country which aim at bringing the Uniform Civil Code into the picture as it is believed that with the advent of such a code, there would be lesser religious tension between communities and they will operate on a much more peaceful manner. The Constituent Assembly Debates provide a lot of insight as to the merits and demerits of having such a code in reality backed with solid reasonings and therefore, whenever discussions take place, these debates and the keynote speakers are brought to attention in order to understand the rationale and take a final call on the same before any decision can be taken on it. Article 44 still continues to be a vestigial part of the Constitution which sparks debates from time to time but no national action has been taken on it nor it has been implemented in any concrete manner until now.

C. Bills Proposed

When looked at from the perspective of Nehru, 'secularism' refers to neutral tolerance towards all religions and not separation of religions, however, a universalist perspective exists so as to reduce religion from ascending in the society at large [40]. In the Indian Constitution, of 1950 religious individuals were recognized and not the communities, this was because the right to freedom of conscience and the right to freely profess, practice and propagate religion is contained within Article 25 and that applies to individuals [41]. In the interest of modernizing the state, the main effort was made to enact the Hindu Code Bill. This Hindu Code Bull was pronounced with the intention to provide for a civil code which would contain and become a single body of all Hindu personal laws, and it was amended by the British authorities to some extent. In April 1948, this Bill was produced before the Constituent Assembly where many debates and concerns were raised relating to the same and ultimately, it was broken down into three parts which were more specialized in nature that came before the Lok Sabha in 1952 [42]. With the help of the Hindu Marriage Bill, polygamy was outlawed and there were provisions introduced with regard to inter-caste marriages which were absent in the first place, this was a step in the direction of codifying a law which within its ambit includes all religions. The Hindu Adoption and Maintenance Bill was also pronounced, and a key highlight was the adoption of girls, which was not very common until that time along with the Hindu Succession Bill which placed daughters on an equal pedestal as widows and sons and the inheritance concept was made clear when ancestral property was being talked about [43].

The above-mentioned Bills faced a lot of opposition from Hindu nationalists, the leader of Hindu Mahasabha Mr. N.C. Chatterjee and S.P. Mukherjee also vehemently protested the bills as they thought that these bills were dangerous for the integrity and stability of the Hindu society and the traditional forms of marriage that were in existence at the point in time [44]. The major reasoning behind these protests was the fact that only Hindus were being covered under these Bills and the civil reform in the country whereas Article 44 of the Constitution had clearly stated that there would be a Uniform Civil Code formed in the country by the efforts of the Government and these bills were not in furtherance of that Article [45]. A lot of allegations were thrown at the government based on the fact that they did not make any effort to reform or make a bill inclusive of Muslim personal laws and the agenda was only to consider Hindu laws which shows the disparity in the government's decision making, which is not acceptable in any manner whatsoever. Critics also believed that the idea of Nehru and secularism that he was proposing was suffering from a disparity because a smoother treatment was being allotted to Indian Muslims so they feel that they are not being treated in a manner which is not generous and that they feel safe living in independent India, even then Nehru kept his stand and made sure that these bills continued to stay in the picture and this was a powerful move in his attempt to defy the polarized views of Hindu nationalists who believed that this step was in the wrong direction [46].

When one looks at the Hindu Code Bill, a simple observation can be drawn that it is not homogenous and even after the Bill has been enacted, not all Hindus are being covered under the same and a similar case exists with Christians and Muslims as well, under their personal laws [47]. Due to hefty debates and criticisms which were faced during the drafting of these bills, it was believed that the 3 acts which were launched as a part of the Hindu Code were diluted to a great extent so that there is no debate against it and the population is satisfied with these laws. Faizan Mustafa who is a constitutional scholar took this Hindu Code under consideration and provided his views to state that, there were many fallacies in the Bill, like the Hindu Marriage Act prohibits marriages amongst close relatives, it is still considered as an auspicious marriage in many Hindu communities across India and similarly in the case of Succession Act, a long battle was fought until daughters were included as coparceners in the ambit of the act [48]. He also stated that the tribals of the country continued to follow their own laws as opposed to the existing laws of the country and kept themselves separate from it therefore, the concept of no-fault and uniformity in the Hindu Code Bill was still lacking [49].

After the changes which were individually made in Hindu and Muslim personal laws between 1950 to 2019, there were no major bills that were proposed and simple deliberations and discussions on the topic continued to take place.

An interesting development happened in the year 2019 when Goa went ahead and adopted a Uniform Civil Code, which was considered one of the most discussed examples in India [50]. The Goa Civil Code was promulgated by the Portuguese in the ear 1867 and it allowed for polygamy in Hindus, however, the Shariat Act of Muslims was not extended to the Muslims of the state of Goa, and they continue to be governed by the Portuguese and

Hindu law which is in place there [51]. A lot of concessions were provided for Catholics as well as they did not have a compulsion of registering their marriages and the priests had the power to dissolve the marriages which have taken place in church, however, it is pertinent to state here that, ground reality and dynamics of state of Goa are very unique and there are multiple cultures which exist there that fostered the implementation of the Civil code that has a lot of legal pluralities to it [52]. In 2019, the BJP government's manifesto and the Uttarakhand Chief Minister's UCC Committee argued on the fact that there should be a Uniform Civil Code in place that should be formed after taking into consideration by taking inputs from all the best practices spread across various religions and fitting them to satisfy the need of the hour today and that would also entail taking up certain practices from the Muslim religion and implementing them to the Bill which applies to Hindus and vice versa, but the question of facing opposition always remains a frontrunner because of which these ideas get rejected at a very nascent stage itself before even reaching maturity [53].

Very recently in 2022, a private bill was introduced in the Rajya Sabha concerning the Uniform Civil Code which had a majority of votes in favour of it [54]. This Bill was seeking to constitute a committee for national inspection and investigation so that a Uniform Civil Code can be prepared and impleFFmented thereafter throughout the territory of India [55]. However, this Bill also met a similar fate to previous others and a leader of the MDMK Party strongly stated that this Bill was basically a weapon which would be used to destroy the minorities in the country and various notices opposing this Bill and its existence were passed [56]. The CPI (M) Party and its members also reiterated the fact that India is a secular country and it promises to provide protection to all sections of people if such a Civil Code is being considered to be implemented in the country, there should be a consultation period that should include taking opinions of all the communities from different religions who would be impacted in case such a Bill comes into power and is enacted [57]. There were some other Members of Parliament who opposed this Bill and stated that this idea is not necessary nor desirable and should be revoked with immediate effect as it would tamper with the very spirit of the Constitution and the rights contained under the same.

Therefore, after having examined the number of Bills that have been proposed for the enactment of the Uniform Civil Code to bring it into power from just being a Directive Principle of State Policy, it can be said with certainty that there have to be more efforts and awareness before a new Bill for the same in presented before the Parliament and for that campaigns need to be held along with getting a fair understanding of what people construe and think of the implementation of such a Bill which would completely reform the laws of the nation. Since India has an extremely diverse population, it goes without saying that there would be both positive and negative views about implementing such a Bill and the views that people hold for it. However, an attempt to examine what the population think has become necessary solely because of the fact that up until now only the decision-making bodies have been discussing it without taking the opinion of those who would be the most affected by it and once their views have been taken, the real picture will be painted and a Bill can be placed before the Parliament which has a backing of public opinions.

D. The Key Contributors

The Uniform Civil Code has seen a development taking place for a very long time and there have been many contributors who have got the progression of the same to the level on which it stands today. Based on the many deliberations and topics under Chapter 2, the major contributors to the Uniform Civil Code will be identified and how they played a role would also be clarified in this section. It can be said that the Portuguese followed by the Britishers were the first ones to start the discussions on the Uniform Civil Code. The Goa Civil Code which exists as of today is a result of the various efforts that were put in by the Portuguese to make it come to life and then the Goa government took inspiration from the same and enacted one in Goa in 2019 which continues to be there. For the rest of India, under British rule which continued for more than 100 years, there were deliberations on the topic of a Uniform Civil Code as they believed it would bring legal reforms in the country for the betterment of India and uniform law would ensure that there is no foul-play. Although it can be assumed that the Britishers must have thought of the Uniform Civil Code as a way out to make administration easier, the discussion was sparked in their ruling days which continues to exist and have a place in the Indian Constitution.

After the British Raj came to an end, a committee under B.N. Rau was also set up to understand and bring in a Uniform Civil Code in the country to bring uniformity [58]. Although not many changes happened due to this Committee, a Hindu Code Bill came into existence which aimed at codifying the Hindu law across various aspects. This was also a momentary step and a great contributor towards the discussions to continue the Uniform Civil Code. After India gained independence, and the task to draft the Constitution began to take place, a Constituent Assembly was set up which had members from different religious backgrounds arguing on all aspects which would form a part of the Constitution and the Uniform Civil Code was also one such topic which was heavily debated during the Constituent Assembly Debates in 1948. The key contributors who spoke for the Bill were Mr. K.M Munshi, Mr. A.K. Ayyar and Honorable Dr. B.R. Ambedkar who gave out points that supported the proposition of having a Uniform Civil Code in place in India. However, the Muslim members of the community were not supporting the motion of passing the Uniform Civil Code as they believed it would hamper the secularity of the state and the personal laws which are existing in the country, these individuals were Mahaboob Ali Baig, Mohammed Ismail, Hussain Imam, B. Pocker Bahadur and M.A. Ayyangar as they debated in a hefty manner so as to ensure that the Uniform Civil Code does not become the norm of the nation and stays as a part of the Directive Principle of State Policy.

Thereafter, the courts played a major role in contributing and shaping the discussions for Uniform Civil Code as they passed the decisions in case of Shah Bano Begum pointed out a recommendation in this direction [59]. Thereafter, multiple points were raised, and the court contributed again to the discussions by pronouncing their decision in the case of Daniel

Latifi [60]. Therefore, it would be baseless to exclude the courts from the list of contributors of the Uniform Civil Code. The Court urged the government to come up with a UCC once again a decade later in a public interest litigation seeking to outlaw the practice of Hindu men abandoning their wives, without lawfully divorcing them and converting to Islam for the sole purpose of marrying a second time [61]. Therefore, the court has acted as a catalyst in these discussions and contributed towards the ongoing discussions.

Although nothing fruitful came out of the courts acting like agents of citizens of India, the deliberations did not come to an end because there is evidence that, till today there are multiple discussions taking place about having the Uniform Civil Code enacted and that too in a manner so it becomes applicable to all population, the evidence of this is the Bill that was introduced in the Parliament very recently in 2022. However, the future of the Bill remained the same as it was for the Bills before because of the very fact that individuals view it as the enforcement of one single law across the nation and do not see the agenda behind it which is very pertinent. There is still a notion that Hindu laws are trying to be implemented on each individual no matter which religious backing they come from, although that is not the case. India is a secular and diverse country will have to make a variety of deliberations before they come forward with the actual Uniform Civil Code that they wish to have in place. All the key contributors to the Uniform Civil Code both the supporters and non-supporters have provided a platform on which there can be discourse, however, when the contributors are fixated on one particular decision without contributing anything towards it then the discussions come to a standstill and the topic cannot proceed ahead. Therefore, to have meaningful discourse in place, discussion must take place on a parliamentary level wherein a committee is set up through which arguments of both sides can be heard and then a final decision can be read. It is not important that at the end of such discussion, the Uniform Civil Code gets implemented but the fact that the discussions were held and were backed by relevant sources and public opinion holds importance. The day this can be achieved, a meaningful discourse and a healthy outcome will be in place.

Apart from all the key contributors who have already been identified through the above discussion, a significant factor that should be considered here is the fear psychology that plays a major role in political science and was therefore reinforced by the immigration of the elite Muslim population directly to Pakistan, while the remaining population remained committed to traditions [62]. The section of the population that was devoid of education services viewed the Sharia law as divine in nature and ignored the ground realities that were associated with the same and its implementation on a practical level [63]. It ultimately resulted in poverty, illiteracy and insecurity amongst the population taking place which thereby led to communal riots throughout the world therefore the process of updating these Sharia laws became completely impossible in nature because of the emotions of the population that were enjoined with the same and it could never travel ahead with the time and continued to remain archaic in nature [64]. Due to the law still being backwards even after the world moved ahead, there was a need which was felt that there should be a uniform law that should be in place and govern all societies alike so that there is no disparity when it comes to the application of laws and the governance of people and masses throughout [65]. Talking about the Hindu side of society as well, they were not open to the change either and did not want a uniform civil code to be implemented which would apply equally everywhere and the innate reason was that there lies a lot of diversity in the entire Hindu population and when diversity is coupled with illiteracy, new changes are not welcomed in an easy way and there is always a hesitation which is encountered because of the only reason that this section of the population wants their beliefs to be safeguarded at all times and do not want that to get affected as a result of any update in the law which is for their own well-being at the end of the day. It was observed by Dr Engineer that the issue of a uniform civil code was being politicized in an extreme manner which is why it could not be implemented and why the parties around the country have different views surrounding the same [66]. The views of Mr Farouqui about Indian Muslims and their identity has a lot of relevance in the global context when looked at broadly as he states that the image of Muslims in India since a very long time back has been unique and being a Muslim comes with a burden of being judged as suspicious and being prejudiced most of the times [67]. The most common dilemma that a Muslim is caught in is between the anti-Muslim movements which are extremely common and the jihadi Muslim pre-notion which leave only two sides for a common Muslim individual to pick from and this is not what they want at every level as this is not they want to be associated with [68]. Now, similar is the case of those Muslims who reside in India and the atmosphere of extremism that they have to face continuously even when India is known to be a secular country which respects and harbours all religions with equal status, dignity and respect. Talking specifically about the Indian situation,

Farouqui points out that when the Indian context is being considered the situation is somewhat different as Muslims form an intrinsic part of the society since time immemorial as Muslims ruled a huge part of India till the time of the British conquest took place and Islam did not remain confined to only a part of the country but was almost everywhere as it permeated its way through the society in every part and also became an important stratum of culture and life throughout India at one point in time [69]. When the British conquest brought a renaissance in Bengal, it failed to do so in the Muslim community and there was no lead taken in that matter hence, the idea of having Pakistan was popularized amongst the entire population which led to a lot of protests on a large scale and the fight for this given cultural hegemony ultimately resulted in the destruction of having a civil society in place which was not an appreciable moment at all in the history of both the uniform civil code as well as that of the country [70]. Mr Farouqui ultimately suggests that the role that is played by the Muslim middle class should be expanded and therefore the poor treatment of Indian Muslims will improve as a result of the same, the voice of the Muslim middle class would be heard with active participation from their end [71]. Dr Tahir Mahmood has quoted in the Shah Bano Case that there should be a uniform civil code that should come into action and be in place and he has drawn a very practical example from the case and related it to that topic to emphasize the ultimate advantage that this code could bring along with it [72]. Dr Mahmood's stand for a uniform civil code has always been very practical and upfront in nature and because his views were being used by extremist groups to popularize their own ideas of violence, he refrained from commenting on that issue completely but the fact remains that he believed and was of the opinion that if such a code is implemented and that there is a uniformity in law it could bring a lot of affirmative changes along which would benefit the entire society and the position of the Muslim population will also be improved drastically. This is not an example of a view which lies in favour of the uniform civil code but the arguments that have been made in favour of the Code have always been practical in nature keeping in mind the aspect of uniformity and absence of communal hatred resulting from differential treatment not consciously but because of the law which is applicable upon them as a result of the traditions and culture that they follow and wish to follow to protect the individuality of their community overall, especially being a part of a secular country like India. Dr Mahmood has always been a very important contributor towards the topic of uniform civil code and why it should be in existence in a country like India where the population is extremely diverse in nature and there are so many subjects which are governed as per laws applicable to various religions and this creates an atmosphere of animosity amongst the population which also leads to riots and communalism taking place which is not at all a healthy occurrence for the country [73]. He not only makes arguments from the perspective of differential laws but also talks about it from the other side as to what would be the advantages of having a similar law that would apply to everyone similarly and would have an equal impact which would also help in lessening the cases like Shah Bano Begum and would ultimately help in achieving some level of gender equality which as of now is not completely there and a huge reason for the same is the nature of the law which is in place and how justice is imparted through courts which are based on these very laws [74]. It is very visible that there cannot be a blanket statement made to state that one law is better than the other, this can only be decided if a given law is enacted for the people and is looking after their well-being at the end of the day and how successful it is in doing the same. Not only the success is an important point but the fact that this law has to take into account the problems which are very commonly encountered with women and do justice to them is also equally important and if this is achieved along with keeping in mind that all communities and their respective laws are catered to, a uniform civil code can be enacted to showcase and prove that one secular country where one of the most diverse set of the population is residing can have one law in place which would be the governing law and that no one would have an issue with the same would be an ideal scenario to be witnessed. Therefore, the above literature that has been elaborated upon was extremely necessary as it is also a key contributor towards the debate on uniform civil code and why it should be in place. These contributors are from both ends the one which lies in favor and the others which are against the implementation however, the one which is in favor entails a lot of great arguments with them that would ultimately help in the progress of the country overall by bringing the much-needed change and helping the masses to be governed in a never before fashion resulting in a more peaceful environment wherein the country would be able to operate.

Notes

1. Krati Sachdev, *Uniform Civil Code,* Legal Service India, https://www.legalserviceindia.com/legal/article-773-uniform-civil-code.html

2. *Id.*

3. *Uniform Civil Code - Challenges, Suggestions and Debate On UCC,* BYJU's., https://byjus.com/free-ias-prep/need-for-a-uniform-civil-code-in-a-secular-india/ (last visited Feb. 10, 2023)

4. *Id.*

5. *Id.*

6. Madhavi Gaur, *What is Uniform Civil Code in India? Know History, articles and more,* Adda 24|7 (Feb. 10, 2023), https://currentaffairs.adda247.com/what-is-uniform-civil-code-in-india/

7. *Id.*

8. *Id.*

9. *Id.*

10. *Supra* note 3, at 1

11. *Id.*

12. *Id.*

13. *Id.*

14. Abhinav Mehrotra, *Uniform Civil Code (UCC) in India: An overview,* Observer Research Foundation (Jan. 06, 2022), https://www.orfonline.org/expert-speak/uniform-civil-code-ucc-in-india-an-overview/

15. *Supra* note 3, at 1

16. *Id.*

17. *Id.*

18. Arun Anand, *How Ambedkar, Munshi & Krishnaswamy Ayyar argued for Uniform Civil Code at Constituent Assembly,* The Print (Nov. 26, 2021), https://theprint.in/india/how-ambedkar-munshi-krishnaswamy-ayyar-argued-for-uniform-civil-code-at-constituent-assembly/771945/

19. *Id.*

20. *Id.*

21. *Id.*

22. CONSTITUENT ASSEMBLY DEBATES, November 23, 1948 *speech by* MAHBOOB ALI BAIG, available at https://www.constitutionofindia.net/constitution_assembly_debates/volume/7/1948-11-23 (Last visited on February 11, 2023)

23. *Id.*

24. CONSTITUENT ASSEMBLY DEBATES, November 23, 1948 *speech by* B. POCKER SAHIB BAHADUR, available at https://www.constitutionofindia.net/constitution_assembly_debates/volume/7/1948-11-23 (Last visited on February 11, 2023)

25. *Id.*

26. *Id.*

27. CONSTITUENT ASSEMBLY DEBATES, November 23, 1948 *speech by* HUSSIAN IMAM, available at https://www.constitutionofindia.net/constitution_assembly_debates/volume/7/1948-11-23 (Last visited on February 11, 2023)

28. *Id.*

29. *Id.*

30. *Id.*

31. CONSTITUENT ASSEMBLY DEBATES, November 23, 1948 *speech by* M.A. AYYANGAR, available at https://www.constitutionofindia.net/constitution_assembly_debates/volume/7/1948-11-23 (Last visited on February 11, 2023)

32. CONSTITUENT ASSEMBLY DEBATES, November 23, 1948 *speech by* K.M. MUNSHI, available at https://www.constitutionofindia.net/constitution_assembly_debates/volume/7/1948-11-23 (Last visited on February 11, 2023)

33. *Id.*

34. *Id.*

35. CONSTITUENT ASSEMBLY DEBATES, November 23, 1948 *speech by* A.K. AYYAR, available at https://www.constitutionofindia.net/constitution_assembly_debates/volume/7/1948-11-23 (Last visited on February 11, 2023)

36. *Id.*

37. *Id.*

38. CONSTITUENT ASSEMBLY DEBATES, November 23, 1948 *speech by* DR. B.R. AMBEDKAR, available at https://www.constitutionofindia.net/constitution_assembly_debates/volume/7/1948-11-23 (Last visited on February 11, 2023)

39. *Id.*

40. *Nehru And the Hindu Code Bill,* Outlook (Feb. 03, 2022), https://www.outlookindia.com/website/story/nehru-and-the-hindu-code-bill/221000

41. *Id.*

42. *Id.*

43. *Id.*

44. *Id.*

45. *Id.*

46. *Id.*

47. Diksha Munjal, *Explained | The Uniform Civil Code,* The Hindu (Nov. 06, 2022, 10:54PM), https://www.thehindu.com/news/national/explained-the-uniform-civil-code/article66105351.ece

48. *Id.*

49. *Id.*

50. *Id.*

51. *Id.*

52. *Id.*

53. *Id.*

54. Rahul Garg, *Private Bill to Implement Uniform Civil Code Introduced In Rajya Sabha,* Live Law (Dec. 10, 2022, 10:23AM), https://www.livelaw.in/news-updates/private-bill-to-implement-uniform-civil-code-introduced-in-rajya-sabha-216307

55. *Id.*

56. *Id.*

57. *Id.*

58. *Supra* note 6, at 1

59. *Id.*

60. *Id.*

61. *Id.*
62. Shimon Shetreet and Hiram Chodosh, Uniform Civil Code for India, 137-144 (Oxford University Press, 2015)
63. *Id.*
64. *Id.*
65. *Id.*
66. *Id.*
67. *Id.*
68. *Id.*
69. *Id.*
70. *Id.*
71. Tahir Mahmood, Family Law in India (EBC, 2023)
72. *Id.*
73. *Id.*
74. *Id.*

CHAPTER 3

Judicial Pronouncements on Uniform Civil Code

Judiciary has, on multiple occasions, re-iterated the importance of implementing Uniform Civil Code. The judiciary has voiced its support for the establishment of the Uniform Civil Code by Article 44 of the Constitution when we examine a few decided instances. The Court's stance on passing a uniform civil code is based on protecting individuals who are oppressed by the actions of others and on the idea that such a code will aid in fostering national cohesion and integrity. Hence, the present chapter will showcase the judicial opinions which has been opined by different courts in three parts. The first half of the chapter explains the landmark judgement which had dealt directly with the issue of implementation of a uniform code and the second half mentions the contemporary incidents which had recently taken place along with the judicial jurisprudence on the same.

The desirability of the code has been stated time and again by various authorities including the apex and other High courts. There is catena of judgements in which the courts have minced no meat in putting forwards the dire need of the implementation of UCC in the country.

Earlier in the year 1951, the Bombay High court delivered a judgment titled as ***The State of Bombay v. Narasu Appa Mali*** [1] the petitioner challenged the validity of the Bombay Prevention of Bigamous Hindu Marriages Act, 1946, which expresses that bigamous relationships void and condemn polygamy among Hindus. The issue before the court was that whether the personal laws are subject to Fundamental Rights guaranteed under the Constitution (Article 13) and what is the constitutional legitimacy of the Bombay Prevention of Hindu Bigamous Marriage Act, 1957 considering article 14, 15 and 25 of the constitution. The court while deciding the issue stated that,

"Article 44 itself recognises separate and distinctive personal laws because it lays down as a directive to be achieved that within a measurable time, India should enjoy the privilege of a common uniform Civil Code applicable to all its citizens irrespective of race or religion. Therefore, what the Legislature has attempted to do by the Hindu Bigamous Marriages Act is to introduce social reform in respect of a. particular community

having its own personal law. The institution of marriage is differently looked upon by the Hindus and the Muslims. Whereas to the former it is a sacrament, to the latter it is a matter of contract. That is also the reason why the question of the dissolution of marriage is differently tackled by the two religions." [2]

While deliberating upon the matter, the court further pointed that,

"In several respects their provisions are mixed up with and are based on considerations of religion and culture; so that the task of evolving a uniform civil code applicable to the different communities of this country is not very easy. The framers of the Constitution were fully conscious of these difficulties and so they deliberately refrained from interfering with the provisions of the personal laws at this stage but laid down a directive principle that the endeavour most hereafter be to secure a uniform civil code throughout She territory of India. It is not difficult to imagine that some of the members of the Constituent Assembly may have felt impatient to achieve this ideal immediately; but as Article 44 shows this impatience was tempered by considerations of practical difficulties in the way That is why the Constitution contents itself with laying down the directive principle in this article." [3]

As regarding the issue presented before the bench, the court observed that the personal laws would not be covered under the ambit of Article

13(3) of the Constitution of India and the act in contention does not discriminate against Hindus. However, the decision of the court that personal laws would not fall within the ambit of article 13(3) was later struck down by the apex court in the case of ***Indian Young Lawyers Association and Ors. v. The State of Kerala and Ors*** [4]

In the case of ***Ms. Jorden Diengdeh v. S.S. Chopra*** [5], the Apex Court was presented with the issue of uniformity in personal marriage laws. The Apex Court noted that there is no uniformity at all in the legislation about marriage, such as judicial separation or divorce. Additionally, it emphasised the requirement that the same rules apply in all circumstances, regardless of faith, in instances of irretrievable collapse of marriage and mutual agreement for divorce. When the Court ordered that a copy of its judgement be forwarded to the Ministry of Law and Justice, it brought up the need for creating the Uniform Code for marriage and divorce.

Whilst concluding the judgment, the court parted with much needed reform in the arena of personal laws. The Apex Court, very categorically stated that,

"It is thus seen that the law relating to judicial separation, divorce and nullity of marriage is far, far from uniform. Surely the time has now come for a complete reform of the law of marriage and to make a uniform law applicable to all people irrespective of religion or caste. It appears to be necessary to introduce irretrievable break down of marriage and mutual consent as grounds of divorce in all cases. We suggest that the time has come for the intervention of the legislature in these matters to provide for a uniform code of marriage and divorce and to provide by law for a way out of the unhappy situations in which couples like the present have find themselves in."

Since the chapter revolves around the judicial opinion on the matter, it is vital to start the discussion with the judgment of ***Mohd. Ahmed Khan v. Shah Bano Begum*** [6]. It is a landmark judgement on the issue of UCC as while pronouncing the judgment, the constitutional bench observed that it is a harsh reality that the article containing the provision for Uniform Civil Code had remained a dead letter of law. The bench stated that "it is the State which is charged with the duty of securing a uniform civil code for the citizens of the country and, unquestionably, it has the legislative competence to do so" [7]

It is also a significant judgement as the constitutional bench put the constitutional principles in higher pedestal than religious laws and held that the provision for maintenance under section 125 of Code of Criminal Procedure, 1973 (hereinafter referred as Cr.P.C) applies to all citizens, regardless of religion. In this case, Shah Bano was divorced by her husband after 40 years of marriage, and she sought maintenance under Section 125 of the Cr.P.C. It was opined that she was entitled to maintenance from her husband, who possesses sufficient resources to sustain her and their children. The Supreme Court stated that religion professed by a spouse or spouses has no place in S. 125 of the Cr.P.C. because it provides a measure based on social justice for an individual's obligation. It should be noted that the Supreme Court had previously expressed a similar viewpoint in several cases prior to this one. However, the Supreme Court's decision in Shah Bano's case sparked outrage, controversy, and a nationwide debate among Muslims, who expressed their displeasure. The resentment against this verdict was so much so that to nullify the effect of this judgement, a separation legislation was passed by the parliament to appease the agitated sections of the society. It can thus be stated that the Supreme Court's decision in Shah Bano's case can be viewed through the lens of establishing uniformity of law of maintenance by applying the provisions of Section 125 of the Cr.P.C. equally to all citizens of India, regardless of religion.

The abundance of personal laws, often, are used to escape the uniform laws, which otherwise would not have been possible. The case of Sarla Mudgal is a perfect example of disadvantages and loopholes that persist due to the presence of several personal laws. In the case of **_Sarla Mudgal v. Union of India_** [8], bench made certain serious statements regarding Uniform Civil Code.

The case was a consolidation of four writ petitions filed in the Supreme Court. Here, the main contention before the court was to examine the issue that whether a person who has already married in accordance with the rituals of one religion, can solemnise second marriage in other religion, in order to escape the consequences of first marriage. In addition to it, in such conditions, whether the first marriage would be considered to be dissolved and what would be the liability of the husband with respect to his first wife. Here, the husband had embraced Islam in order to remarry another woman, since the religious practices of Islam allows marriage up to four wives legal.

The case widely discussed the implementation of article 44. It has been categorically stated,

"A common Civil Code will help the cause of national integration by removing disparate loyalties to laws which have conflicting ideologies. No community is likely to bell the cat by making gratuitous concessions on this issue. It is the State which is charged with the duty of securing a uniform civil code for the citizens of the country and, unquestionably; it has the legislative competence to do so." [9]

The percept that a secular state should constitute a law that applies to every citizen equivocally, was the main intention behind including article 44 in the Indian Constitution. The court held that a citizen who converts to other religion may be prohibited from getting remarried by law unless he first gets a divorce from his previous spouse. State shall take this endeavour of making uniform laws on such matters and such provisions should be applicable on everyone, regardless of whether they are a Hindu, Muslim, Christian, Sikh, Jain, or Buddhist. To prevent conflicts of interest after death, provisions for maintenance, succession, and other matters should be made.

Similar judgement, based on the issue of bigamy by the case title of ***Lily Thomas v. Union of India*** [10] was also pronounced. The need of Uniform Civil Code was amplified by the Hon'ble apex court. The need and desirability of a uniform code in the Indian scenario was highlighted by the court. However, the court also accepted the fact that since Directive Principles cannot be sought to be enforced by challenging them before the court, the bench can only request the government to look into the matter of implementation of a uniform code.

Through various cases, the pertinent question of who bears the wait of bringing forward a uniform code governing the personal laws, was presented before the courts of the country. It has been observed that the court has expressed the pressing need of bringing such laws in their observations however, such observations were seldom found to be cloaked with the need of legislature to act, as bringing such laws is the policy discretion of the legislature.

In the case of ***Ahmedabad Women Action Group (AWAG) and others v. Union of India*** [11], the Apex Court was presented with the issues pertaining to the polygamy. The court through this judgment decided three writ petitions presented before it. The main issue before the court was whether such laws must be enacted by the legislature of the country, and can be applied uniformly to everyone. Another substantial issue that was put forth before the apex court to decide was whether the judicial courts should have any kind of interference in the matters pertaining to the unification of the personal laws or not. [12]

In its judgement, the court presented an affirmative stance pertaining to the introduction of such laws, however, court also commented that such laws should not be introduced or implemented in one go as it would be much sudden of a change. As it is stated earlier that this affirmative stance of the court was coupled with the concern of it being a purely policy decision. [13]

Ultimately the court stated that,

"The Court at the very outset commented that these Writ Petitions do not deserve disposal on merits in as much as the arguments advanced before it wholly involves issues of State policies with which the Court will not ordinarily have any concern. Further, Court found that when similar attempts were made, of course by others, on earlier occasions this Court held that the remedy lies somewhere else and not by knocking at the doors of the courts." [14]

Moving further, in the case of **_Pragati Varghese v. Cyril George Varghese_** [15], the Indian Divorce Act, 1869's Section 10 was deemed unconstitutional by the Bombay High Court. This Section stipulates that when a Christian wife files for divorce on grounds of desertion or cruelty, she had to prove adultery along with the other mentioned grounds.

The Indian Divorce Act, 1869's Section 10 was declared unlawful by the Bombay High Court because it infringes a Christian woman's fundamental right to live with dignity under Article 21 of the Constitution. The Court pointed out that

Section 10 of the Act forces the woman to cohabitate with a man who has abandoned her or mistreated her. Hence there is denial on the part of legislation, for dissolving a marriage that has already broken down. Such legislative practices cannot be encouraged. According to Article 21 of the Constitution, the Bombay High Court's ruling protects a Christian woman's human dignity and accords her honour while she lives with her husband and files for divorce on the grounds of his desertion or cruelty.

One may argue the relevancy of this judgement with the idea of having a uniform civil code. However, the case is a suitable example of the tyranny posed by the multiple personal laws. Though, the idea of UCC has not been discussed explicitly in the judgement, but the idea that yardstick of constitutional principles, which must be followed, without taking into consideration whether the laws belong to religious practices or any other customs, is synonymous with the concept of UCC.

Similarly, in the case of ***John Vallamattom & Anr. v. Union of India*** [16], the apex court again stated its view on the codification of a uniform civil law. The petitioners challenged the constitutionality of Section 118 of the Indian Succession Act of 1925, claiming that it was discriminatory under Article 14 and violated Articles 25 and 26 of the Constitution of India. S. 118 of the Act addresses a Christian's ability to bequeath his property for religious or charitable purposes. This Section limited a Christian's right to make a bequest if he has a nephew, niece, or any other relative. The term relative includes an adopted son but not the testator's wife. The Court ruled that Section 118 of the Succession Act is unconstitutional because it violates Article 14 of the Constitution.

The Court also stated that Articles 25 and 26 of the Constitution of India, do not apply in this case because the disposition of property for religious and charitable purposes is not an essential part of the Christian religion. These Articles only safeguard rituals and ceremonies that are fundamental to religion. Based on the Court's decisions in the aforementioned cases, it is evident that the judiciary is in favour of enacting a common civil Code in order to eliminate religious ideologies-based differences, prevent abuse of personal laws, and promote national integration.

Further, the landmark case of ***Seema v. Ashwini Kumar***, [17] which was delivered by division bench of Supreme Court, deals with the issue of consequences of non-registration of marriages. The bench categorically laid down the essentiality of registration of a marriage irrespective of the religion which is adhered by the parties. As per the judgement, all marriages should be registered. The court, through its judgement, also ordered the Centre and State governments to amend the existing laws or to enact new rules regarding the afore-mentioned and notify accordingly within three months. The Court also stated that the rules enacted would remain in effect until the respective governments enacted legislation mandating marriage registration.

The aforementioned Supreme Court decision is a significant step towards enacting a Uniform Civil Code. Many cases have been reported in which husbands abandon their respective wives, refuse marriages in order to avoid liability to support their wives and children, and also to deny them the right to inherit their property. The Supreme Court's decision has broader implications for preventing such evil motives of irresponsible husbands, because as a result of this decision, i.e., due to marriage registration, several good things can happen that may maintain healthy family relations. For example, fraud committed by either spouse during the marriage by concealing or misrepresenting his or her age can be avoided.

Moving to the recent judicial pronouncements, Justice Pratibha M. Singh, Delhi High Court, during the hearing of an appeal made stern remarks on the lackadaisical implementation approach over UCC. The matter was related to setting aside of a divorce decree by family court due to conflict between the regulating personal laws on the matter. The single judge bench remarked that,

"In modern Indian society, which is gradually becoming homogenous, the traditional barriers of religion, community and caste are slowly dissipating. The youth of India belonging to various communities, tribes, castes or religions who solemnize their marriages ought not to be forced to struggle with issues arising due to conflicts in various personal laws, especially in relation to marriage and divorce." [18]

The bench further remarked that,

"The need for a Uniform Civil Code as envisioned under Article 44, has been reiterated from time to time by the Supreme Court. Cases like the present one repeatedly highlights the need for such a Code - 'common to all', which would enable uniform principles being applied in respect of aspects such as marriage, divorce, succession etc., so that settled principles, safeguards and procedures can be laid down and citizens are not made to struggle due to the conflicts and contradictions in various personal laws." [19]

Very recently the Hijab controversy, agitated the masses and stirred up the debate on UCC. Originated with the same controversy of the extent of regulation and interference of authority of state in religious practices of the masses, UCC and Hijab issue share the same religious resistance. The matter sprouted with the tussle between uniformity in the dress code for students and the religious practise of wearing hijab in the classrooms. The controversy arose when Karnataka Government banned Hijab in educational institutions. The mater reached to the High court where petitioner stated that it is direct violation of their right to practice their religion as wearing Hijab is essential religious practice in Islam. [20] Karnataka High Court upheld the restriction on Hijab, stating that prescription of a school uniform by the state is a reasonable restriction the students' rights under Article 25. The verdict was challenged in Supreme Court and the matter is listed for hearing in the upcoming days.

The question looms on the face of Indian governance, that what is the intersection point of faith and law, and to what extent the state's interference is allowed when it comes to religious arena. These incidents imply State's submission to whims of personal laws instead of suprema lex, i.e., the constitution of India. This controversy has again stirred up a similar debate, what should be put first; a common and unequivocal provisions applicable to all or personal religious practices.

Since the petitions of challenging intersection of religion and law are being discussed, it would be pertinent to mention a petition that has been filed to the apex court stating that the right to equality and dignity is being violated by certain Muslim personal laws. Sameena Begum and other Muslim women petitioned the Supreme Court in 2018 to overturn various Muslim personal laws concerning divorce and marriage. Through their petition, they challenged the practises of polygamy and nikah halala on the ground that they violate the rights to equality, non-discrimination, and dignity of Muslim women. [21]

The prayer that was sought through this petition was regarding declaration of applicability of sections of Indian Penal Code, 1860 (i.e., s. 375, 498A, on the matters of Polygamy, Nikah Halala and Triple Talaq. In addition to it, the petitioner also sought to declare s. 2 of Muslim Personal Law (*Shariyat*) Application Act, 1937 unconstitutional (only to the extent where the act declares the practices of polygamy and Nikah Halala as valid).

This petition along with four other petitions were tagged by the Supreme Court. Later, the matter was referred to constitution bench (constituting of 5 apex court judges). The hearing on the matter is still pending before the bench.

Similarly, a bunch of petitions have also been filed in Supreme Court seeking uniformity in laws pertaining to succession, inheritance, age of marriage, guardianship, and adoption. These petitions are most recent attempt made to get a favourable order from the apex court considering the slow approach of the legislative authorities.

Lawyer and politician Ashwini Upadhyay of the ruling party filed these petitions. The petitioner claims that these laws violate the gender justice and religious equality established by Articles 14 and 15 of the Constitution. Furthermore, he contends that these regulations offend women's dignity, which is safeguarded by their article 21 right to life and liberty. Initially, a three-judge bench consisting of Chief Justice S.A. Bobde, Justices A.S. Bopanna, and V. Ramasubramanian heard the petitions. The petitions are listed for hearing before the hon'ble apex court.

In dealing with a batch of petitions concerning the issue of an interfaith marriage contracted by the petitioners and seeking court protection, the Allahabad High Court urged the government to act on the issue of UCC implementation. [22] The court stated that,

"The UCC is a necessity and mandatorily required today. It cannot be made 'purely voluntary' as was observed by Dr. B.R. Ambedkar 75 years back, in view of

the apprehension and fear expressed by the members of the minority community." [23]

The Supreme Court bench consisting of Chief Justice DY Chandrachud and Justice PS Narasimha declined to hear a public interest litigation (PIL) challenging the decision of the states of Uttarakhand and Gujarat to form committees to introduce and implement the Uniform Civil Code (UCC). Mr. Anoop Baranwal had filed the PIL in question. While observing that the concerned states had the right to form or constitute committees under Article 162 of the Indian Constitution, the bench concluded that the PIL lacked merit.

The judgment of ***Paulo Coutinho v. Maria Luiza Valentina Pereira Case*** [24] is of a recent origin. Delivered in the year 2019, the presents perfect picture of the lackadaisical attitude towards the implementation of UCC. The judgment authored by the then Chief Justice of India, Dipak Misra, stated that there is serious lack of attempts made towards consolidation and implementation of much awaited and promised uniform code. The Apex Court outrightly stated that,

"It is interesting to note that whereas the founders of the Constitution in Article 44 in Part IV dealing with the Directive Principles of State Policy had hoped and expected that the State shall endeavour to secure for the citizens a Uniform Civil Code throughout the territories

of India, till date no action has been taken in this regard. Though Hindu laws were codified in the year 1956, there has been no attempt to frame a Uniform Civil Code applicable to all citizens of the country despite exhortations of this Court in the case of Mohd. Ahmed Khan v. Shah Bano and Sarla Mudgal & Ors. vs. Union of India & Ors."

Past year, the Uttarakhand government formed a Committee of Experts to examine the relevant laws governing personal civil matters of Uttarakhand residents and to prepare draught laws/laws or suggest changes to existing laws on the subject, which includes marriage, divorce, property rights, succession/inheritance, adoption, maintenance, custody, and guardianship. The Committee was also tasked with producing a report on the implementation of a Uniform Civil Code in Uttarakhand. The Committee is chaired by former Supreme Court Justice Ranjana Prakash Desai.

The judiciary has several times intervened with the injustices caused by tyranny in the garb of personal laws. However, if the pronouncement had fall short on the political expectations of the governing party, the same has been overturned by way bringing a legislation negating the effect of the judgement. The extent of proportional application of such Uniform code to various communities has not been determined by the courts. Codification of such laws will require extensive deliberation and discussion from each community. Implementation of the same will also be met with resistance from certain factions of the society, however, the process should not be pushed for further dates merely because of that reason. Keeping in view the constitutional mandate, the present government should act fast upon the matter rather than adopting a lackadaisical approach.

Given India's diverse social fabric, implementing the Uniform Civil Code throughout the entire nation is a mammoth effort. The concept of such a unified code could only be given a practical form when the contentions of all the stakeholders and religious scholars are considered keeping in view the delicate balance between the right to practise a religion and enacting a uniform civil law.

Code is not a demand for Hindus, Muslims, Christians, or Parsis. It would be futile to assert religious agenda upon the need for such code. It is rather for the recognition of all women's human rights. It can be said that the time has come, when this issue must be seen without the tinted glasses of religious appeasement. The central and the sole motivating force behind the need of UCC is the elimination of discrimination and establishment of constitutional spirit of equality and reasonableness.

Ideologies of various religions and the right of any person to practise and propagate religions would not stand in the way of the creation of a Uniform Civil Code because religious ideologies and the right to religion stand on a different foundation than a Uniform Civil Code because a Uniform Civil Code is entirely secular. Law uniformity would be guaranteed to all Indian citizens, regardless of their religious beliefs. Such uniformity would have no negative impact on the Fundamental Right to Religion guaranteed by Articles 25 to 28 of the Constitution. For example, family matters affecting all communities, such as marriage, maintenance, custody of children, divorce, succession, and so on, can be addressed by uniform law.

Thus, to conclude we need to understand the importance and the need the urgent enactment of the uniform civil code. The time has come to place all personal laws of all religions under a stringent check and discard all laws that are found to violate the Constitution. Personal laws of all religions discriminate against women on matters of marriage, divorce, inheritance and so on. There is an urgent need to carve out the just and equitable laws of all religions and form a blueprint for a uniform civil code based on gender justice and ensure the principle of equality enshrined by our

Constitution and to alter laws which are discriminatory and biased.

The concept of Uniform Civil Code is embedded in the concept of Secularism. Secularism is a principle that requires in-depth analysis, especially when it is coupled with the need of unification of personal laws. Secularism may be interpreted in many ways, and on the altar of all these interpretations, in which the UCC is both exalted and criticised. While certain groups in our society view the UCC as anti-secular, others see it as a sign of secularism and social peace. Last but not least, the UCC is heavily influenced by the issue of Indian women's human rights. Therefore, it is important to comprehend if personal laws are uniform will definitely result in the equal standing of women in society or would merely remain a community aim.

In this context, it can be stated that personal laws in Indian context continue to affect the lives and rights of a large number of women from all communities, leaving them in a very disadvantaged position. Although various efforts are being initiated and undertaken to ensure gender equality through the introduction of international instruments, reforms of national laws, changing trends in judicial pronouncement, recommendations of Law Commissions and other social elite groups, women in our country are still not treated equally and discriminated in the field of family law, particularly in cases of marriage, divorce, maintenance, inheritance, and so on. For long, a gender-neutral code is required in these situations. Hence, the introduction of a uniform civil code is extremely imperative to eliminate discrimination against women regardless of their religion or community, and, eventually, to make our national legislation in conformity with international instruments that are legally enforceable on India through various international conventions and international Human Rights instruments that India has ratified. The time has come for us to try to bring the concept of a Uniform Civil Code to light. Towards the end, it can be stated that for citizens of different religions, it is imperative that for the promotion of national unity and solidarity, as well as for the promotion of national integration, a unified code is an absolute necessity on which no compromise can be made. Different religious streams must merge to reach a common goal, and some unified principles must emerge in the true spirit of Secularism. India requires a unified family law code that incorporates all of its constituent religions. Whether it is the State's endeavour, the mandate of the court, or the Will of the People, only time will tell.

Notes

1. AIR 1952 Bom 84.
2. *Id.*
3. *Ibid.*
4. (2019) 11 SCC 1.
5. (1985) 3 SCC 62
6. 1985 AIR 945
7. Ibid.
8. A.I.R. 1995 S.C. 1531.
9. Ibid.
10. A.I.R. 2000 S.C. 1651.
11. A.I.R. 2000 S.C. 1651
12. Id.
13. Id.
14. Id.
15. AIR 1997 Bom 349.
16. Writ Petition (civil) 242 of 1997.
17. Transfer Petition (civil) 291 of 2005.
18. Satprakash Meena v. Alka Meena, C.R.P.1/2021 and CM APPL. 332/2021.
19. Ibid.
20. Resham and Anr v. The State of Karnataka, W.P. NO.2347 OF 2022
21. Sameena Begum v. Union of India, W.P. (civil) No, 222/2018

22. Marya alias Vaishnavi v. State of UP & others, Writ No. 14896 of 2021.

23. Ibid.

24. Civil Appeal No. 7378 of 2010.

CHAPTER 4

International Perspective Concerning UCC

Introduction:

This chapter presents a bird's eye view of the international perspective concerning the UCC (though not technically in the same spirit as demanded in India, but broadly in the same essence- a unified law applicable to all nationals of a country). What are all the counties where such laws have been introduced, or an attempt is being made to introduce such laws; how is the reception where such laws have already been introduced or their net effect on the legal system of the concerned nations; whether a success or a failure? These are a few questions, in the backdrop of which this chapter will proceed.

In our day, which has become increasingly characterized by a non-Western legal mindset and ideas of being associated with something greater than state-made law, Eurocentric presumptions about value-neutral law have failed terribly. Take a look around the globe. The majority of nations have a system of personal law, even though all may not admit it [1]. However, that is not the end of it.

Law and society are intertwined across the world. Nations with "mixed" legal systems have a number of exemptions for particular communities. Such exceptions are made even in nations that advertise having standardized family laws. When 'ethnic implantation' of new immigrant groups alters a nation's demographic makeup, legal homogeneity then turns into a handy legal illusion [2]. This illustrates an incorrect understanding of the legislation itself. Since we now understand how easily freedom of contract benefits those with the authority to determine the terms, these contract-based interpretations of the law as administered by states are no longer considered a guarantee of human advancement. However, it does not mean that a step towards the same is a step in a bad direction altogether. The question is not about whether to move in that direction or not, rather it is about how and at what pace it should be done. Whether it should be done mechanically in the name in advancement or should it be done with prudence taking the sentiments of the large populous involved.

Earliest Attempts at Unification of Law:

The Romans are directly responsible for the theory of civil law. Roman doctrines were employed to create a code specific to the Roman populace that governed how legal disputes would be resolved. They gave it the name Jus Civile, a legal term used today that supports all legal norms and principles derived from Roman laws and practices, as opposed to those derived from universal customs known as jus gentium or from the fundamental moral principles inherent in human nature, known as jus naturale. It was created by Emperor Justinian, who ascended to the throne in 527 CE. Roman law continued to be used in many other nations despite being interpreted, evolved, and adjusted to [3].

France's civil code is among the most well-known in the world today in a modern sense. Although the unification of previous civil law had started more than a decade earlier, the Napoleon Civil Code was first implemented in France in 1804 and replaced more than 300,000 provincial civil law codes. It encompassed a wide range of topics including property, commodities, usufructs, easements, succession, wills, gifts, contracts, and quasi-contracts, and supplanted both customary law and pre-existing legal rules. The French Code aims to strike a balance between privilege and equality, as well as between traditions and the law [4].

Current Trend towards unified Laws vis-à-vis Case study of Different Nations:

- **Unification movement in USA**

There are several layers of legislation that apply individually to the nation, the state, the county, or agencies and cities in the United States, where the issue of diversity may be more in line with Indian circumstances. States are autonomous legal entities with their own Supreme Courts that adhere to their own customs and laws. Even though these civil laws in the United States are governed by basic principles that apply equally across the country. The Federal Supreme Court only deals with matters of a federal nature or those that impact the entire nation, such as security, taxation, general legal issues, etc [5].

In the U.S.A, a proposed package of laws for state adoption is known as a uniform act. Each state has its collection of laws, some of which are specific to the state or territory while others are the same or almost the same in most states. For instance, each state has its laws governing how its citizen should conduct themselves at home i.e. family laws. The U.S. Constitution places restrictions on the federal government's authority to standardize legal matters between states, even though federal laws can accomplish this. As a result, the Uniform Law Commission (hereinafter referred to as the ULC) - a group of lawyers and policymakers, creates proposed legislation that each state may or may not embrace [6].

The ULC has created several standard acts in the area of family law. However, a lot of governments prefer not to enact such proposed standard acts. For instance, only five states have adopted the Uniform Parentage Act. This chapter addresses a few such uniform laws.

Uniform Child Custody Jurisdiction and Enforcement Act (hereinafter referred to as the uniform child custody Act):

The Uniform Child Custody Act lays forth the footprint that states must follow to recognize and uphold the child custody rulings of other states. Generally, a state court can legally oblige a citizen if it has personal jurisdiction over them. Now what does the term 'personal jurisdiction' mean? Persons who have a physical presence in the state or interact sufficiently with it so that a court's authority over them would be consistent with established standards of justice and fairness are subject to personal jurisdiction by state courts. [7]

Earlier, to abuse law, a parent might avoid having a state court's custody order by juggling across state lines. So, by doing so, a parent could evade the repercussions of breaking the terms of a custody agreement. The same is also termed "parental abduction."

The Uniform Child Custody Act addressed the same issue by permitting state courts to continue to have jurisdiction over a custody decision they made. Legally mandating such parents to give back the child to their home state, it provides that other state courts must recognize the legitimacy of custody decisions made in another state and empowers them to enforce those decisions. By laying down the procedures to ascertain the child's home state; meeting the given requirements, it also settles conflicting claims of state jurisdiction. Almost all states have given a green signal to such rules [8].

Uniform Child Abduction Prevention Act (hereinafter referred to as UCAP Act)

The UCAP Act was created to address parental abduction cases, much like the aforementioned Act. But as it was introduced subsequent to the earlier Act, it offers extra resources to help with situations of child abduction prevention. Under this Act, state courts may apply legal sanctions to prevent a parent from trying to take their child out of the state to avoid having to abide by the conditions of a custody agreement. Few states have given a green signal to the same [9].

Notably, the issue of parental abduction is not limited to just one Nation. The "Hague Abduction (child) Convention" is a global pact that various nations signed in the wake of the said issue. It settles conflicting jurisdictional claims for child custody between various sovereign states, just like the aforementioned Act does. This enables courts in one nation to enforce custody decisions made by courts in another nation and to compel the reunification of children who were unjustly taken from their place of origin. Additionally, the UCAP Act offers legal safeguards that underpin the said Convention on child abduction [10].

Additionally, this Act empowers courts to impose travel restrictions, enrolling a child in the Child Passport Issuance Alert Programme run by the U.S. State Department, requiring foreign parents to acquire a domestic custody order with the same conditions as current custody orders.

Uniform Interstate Family Support Act (hereinafter referred to as the UIFS Act):

Child support orders are another area where jurisdictional issues between state courts are challenging. Earlier, parents would try to get out of paying child support by relocating to another state. Congress passed federal legislation in 1996 that made compliance with the UIFS Act a requirement for states seeking federal assistance for child support enforcement efforts. As a result, its requirements have been enacted by all states and territories in the United States. It places restrictions on a state court's ability to change, uphold, or end a child support obligation. It also offers a procedure for settling competing jurisdictional claims when parents who reside in separate states have child support concerns to resolve. [11]

- **Position in UK**

On two major levels, divorce practices among racial and ethnic minorities in England diverge from those under English law. First off, such minorities usually have religious or cultural conventions that govern divorces. This emphasizes the crucial point made by Pearl and Menskis that, despite the English system's vesting of family law in the state, many racial and ethnic minorities, including Jews and Muslims, traditionally have not turned to the state for these issues. Second, divorces in England "almost always involve obtaining dissolution from a competent court of law," from a procedural standpoint. The majority of the time, ethnic minorities receive divorces outside of court.

The official legislation of the state and the customs of ethnic minorities in England are at odds because of these distinctions [12].

Till 1857, the matters of divorce remained largely in the domain of religious courts, though a decree nullifying a marriage could be obtained from an official court; divorce remained outside their purview. Post that, the divorce rules started to become more lenient, allowing the state to create legislation (exclusively) for the same. Parallel to this, the grounds for divorce were also made more accessible. Consequently, the number of divorce cases went up, especially post the world war era [13].

Marriage irretrievably breaking down was largely pushed as grounds for dissolution of the marriage. It was felt that the law need not sustain a marriage simply because a party was not able to prove an existing ground (fault-based) to obtain a divorce. The Matrimonial Causes Act, 1973 (enacted following the recommendations from the Law Commission in 1966) is the current law on divorce in England; replacing the old grounds for divorce with a single ground - i.e. a marriage has irretrievably broken down. Post 1977, a norm of undefended divorce petitions was introduced thus making a mutual consent divorce a reality (the majority of divorces in England are taken mutually).

The Matrimonial Causes Act, of 1973 governs all matters relating to matrimonial reliefs (including divorce) in England. As Lex Fori, it is an official law of the state governing all its citizens regardless of their religious or cultural preferences with regard to the law's subject matter. The practices of racial and ethnic minorities, however, have presented unique and specific challenges for English courts because of the same rationale that the law should be applied equally in all regions of the country.

The circumstances and norms of ethnic minorities make phrases like "reasonable expectations" and "right-thinking person" (which act as proof of the breakdown of the marriage (a ground for divorce)) in Section 1(2) (b) of the Act, is complex and troublesome. There have been many problematic encounters of the said English law with ethnic minority customs.

In *Ash v. Ash* [14], the court determined that the standard for "behavior" must be objective because the clause utilizes the word "reasonably"; hence, it must be a fact that can be determined by a judge. However, the court ruled that the parties' backgrounds must be considered.

Poulter thinks that courts will be forced to strike a "balance" between fundamental English values and customs approved by the parties, based on "public policy considerations". Another topic that needs to be addressed concerning the ruling on ethnic minority customs is whether or not English courts have shown their competency of making decisions on customs over which they have no cultural or contextual background. We look to two different legal rulings to provide an answer to this topic.

Devi v. Guddu [15] is a case involving Indian Couple living with husband's family. The wife had filed a suit against her husband alleging that her mother-in-law assaulted her. The husband pleaded that charge of cruelty does not hold good against him for something he did not do himself. The court, however, rejected the same. Under English Law, typically, the acts of third parties would not suffice to establish cruelty. However, the Court in this case considered the background and tradition of the extended families of the parties to arrive at the decision. The court, thus, had meaningfully interacted with an ethnic minority practice.

Contrastingly, in ***Khan v. Khan*** [16], the court did not consider the customs of the parties. A husband had forbidden his wife from returning home if she attended a wedding celebration he did not approve of. The court held the husband to be under desertion and did not take account of the custom the wife must obey the husband.

Poulter thinks the choice made in Khan v. Khan was the right one. In a more broad sense, he contends that there must be "limits" on how much cultural diversity is tolerated in England in order to protect the "overriding common good." He argues that "public policy" and "reasonability" are requirements for the court to tolerate the traditions of ethnic minorities, and that "cultural accommodation cannot become a 'cloak for discrimination and bias within the immigrant communities altogether'". One agrees with Poulter's overarching claim that clearly repressive traditions shouldn't be justified. This is especially true in a legal system like the one in England, which has made significant strides in upholding natural justice, gender parity, and other areas [17].

However, English law doesn't seem to have a clear stance on any one branch of Islamic law. That the state is hesitant to acknowledge Muslims as a "racial group" under the Race Relations Act of 1996 is troubling. Many Muslims now feel they are being treated differently than other ethnic minorities as a result of this. According to Carolyn Hamilton, the English legal system has made a number of exclusions for some Christian "dissenter" sects and Jews, allowing them to follow their practices. Other well-known exceptions in English law include those made in the Marriage Act of 1949 with questions relating to the solemnization of marriage for Jews and Quakers. Muslims have not received these considerations.

Even though their rituals appear contrary to treasured and fundamental foundations of English law, highlighting discrimination against Muslims does not automatically justify those customs. On the other hand, the case is made that English law should, as Pearl recommends, engage seriously with Islamic customary practices, and create a precise framework within which such practices can be justified as acceptable or not. According to Pearl and Menski, the current attitude towards Muslim customs appears to be that some practices are acceptable "simply because there is no law against them." Courts have the authority to use the common law's public interest justifications to instantly invalidate practices that up until that moment had not run afoul of the law.

It is hoped that English law would go beyond Khan to deal with ethnic minority customs more honestly and sensitively, especially in previously unexplored areas like Muslim practices. This will not only help British Muslims navigate and anticipate questions of acknowledgement, but it will also help ethnic minority communities develop a stronger sense of connection with the domestic legal system.

Inconsistencies in the Application of legal provisions in Cases of ethnic minorities:

According to Section 5 of the MCA, the divorce petition may be rejected if there would be "grave financial or other hardship" as a result of the divorce. The court, however, must be persuaded before allowing this defence that not only will such "hardship" arise, but also that it would be wrong to dissolve the marriage under any circumstances.

Hindu wives had argued in a number of cases that if their husbands' divorce petitions were granted, it would be a "hardship" for them to return to India. This argument was taken into consideration by the court. The wives attempted to avail the defence under Section 5 of the MCA by asserting that Indian religious and social attitudes on divorce will cause the divorced woman to be shunned and reduced in her community's eyes.

The Court of Appeal determined that this claim would qualify as a case under Section 5 in the case of *Banik v. Banik*. [18] In *Banik v. Banik (No. 2* [19]*)*, the court determined that the divorced wife would not be a social outcast because she would continue to live with her brother's family while being in a situation where she could not remarry. Her defence was therefore ineffective. It is crucial to remember that in cases involving Jews, the comparable traits of "outcaste" and "inability to remarry" to a divorced wife were applied with opposite results.

Similar to the Banik case, the wife was thought to be unlikely to experience societal discrimination as a result of the divorce in *Parghi v. Parghi* [20]. This claim was rejected on the grounds that the parties were Hindus who hailed from affluent and well-educated homes. The court dismissed the hardship defence in *Balraj v. Balraj* [21] on specific grounds. The woman, in this case, lived on the outskirts of Hyderabad, and the court acknowledged that becoming a divorcee would put her in an unusual and unfavorable situation because of her Kshatriya community. However, the court dismissed her argument, ruling that her condition did not meet the criteria for "grave" under Section 5. This was followed by *Rukat v. Rukat* [22], a case involving a Sicilian wife who was Roman Catholic.

The decisions shown above are poor choices. First off, it is assumed that the suffering of a Muslim wife who is given a talaq divorce or a Jewish wife who is an agunah will be more "grave" than that of a Hindu woman in the same situation. A divorced woman is seen quite negatively in many Hindu communities, as Derrett correctly noted. She rarely chooses divorce until her marriage is intolerable [23].

In addition, dowry, a kind of payment, is customarily given to the husband's family by the wife's father (despite the fact that this practice is currently illegal in India). Poulter observes that dowry greed is frequently so intense that young girls are frequently slain if their families cannot satisfy the bridegrooms' families' outrageous dowry demands.

The woman is not allowed to receive her dowry money back if a divorce is granted. She frequently becomes an additional financial strain on her parent's family as a result. This can be especially difficult if the wife's family is struggling financially. In the aforementioned situations, the court seems to have had a very limited understanding of the social environment of a Hindu woman. The contradictory attribution of meanings in a hardship clause to various ethnic minorities raises concerns about a possible element of arbitrary law application. Furthermore, it exhibits some insensitivity toward alleviating human suffering [24].

- **Position in Australia**

Australia does not have a uniform civil code at the federal level. The country follows a system of federalism, where each state and territory has the power to legislate on certain aspects of civil law, including family law, marriage, divorce, and inheritance. As a result, there may be some variations in civil laws across different states and territories in Australia.

For example, family law matters, such as divorce and child custody, are primarily regulated by the Family Law Act 1975 at the federal level. However, each state and territory may have its own legislation on issues such as property division and child protection.

It's important to note that Australia has a secular legal system, meaning that religious laws do not have the same authority as civil laws. While individuals are free to practice their religion, the legal system is based on a common law framework and statutory laws enacted by the federal, state, and territory governments.

However, placing the Australian Aboriginal's customary law within Australia's common law system has been a contentious issue. In cases like ***R v. Sydney Williams (1976)***, [25] courts have given customary sanctions a little window of opportunity. The expansive framework of Australia's Family Law Act clashes awkwardly with the customary personal laws of Jews and Muslims. Jewish women have, for instance, complained that, according to Jewish law, they are forbidden from remarrying and that their children are not allowed to fully participate in their society if their spouse refuses to award "the Gett" (the Get) [26].

Islamic Australians face similar experiences of difficulties with divorce because Sharia law allows a husband extra-judicial divorce. Per contra, to get a divorce, a woman must find a court or other impartial party who will allow the divorce. If she is unable to, she will continue to be considered married in her community and by herself. The experience is similar to that of Jewish women.

- **Position in Canada**

Over 900 separate Indigenous communities, each of which used a unique set of Indigenous legal systems, had their original settlements in what is now Canada. Many people would use their own legal traditions in daily activities such as making contracts, interacting with public and corporate bodies, managing the environment, pursuing criminal charges, and practicing family law. The majority uphold their laws via conventional government combined with elected authorities and federal laws. The legal precedents established through millennia are known through stories, derived from past deeds and replies, as well as through ongoing interpretation by elders and law-keepers — the same method used to create practically all legal traditions, including common laws and civil codes [27].

The field of law known as "aboriginal law" deals with how the government interacts with its indigenous people. According to the Constitutional Act of 1867, the Canadian legislature has the exclusive authority to enact laws pertaining to Aboriginal people, including those who are subject to the Indian Act and other Numbered Treaties as well as those who are not covered by those Acts.

The substance of the legal aspects of marriage and divorce are solely under the purview of the federal government. However, the procedural aspects of the same fall within the sole competence of the provinces. Provinces also have laws governing family care (including spousal maintenance) and marital assets. According to the Canadian Constitution, provincial laws govern inheritance. As a result, each province in Canada has its own set of rules controlling inheritance [28].

Additionally, all provinces in Canada, except for Quebec, have ratified the Personal Property Protection Act (hereinafter referred to as PPS Act), which is founded on the UCC's principles. U.S. debtors frequently choose Canada as their destination because of the application of same.

- **African Stance**

The concept of a uniform civil code in Africa varies across different countries on the continent. While some African countries have implemented certain aspects of a uniform civil code, the extent and implementation vary. One notable example is Tunisia, which adopted a relatively progressive personal status code in 1956, following its independence. The code abolished polygamy, established women's rights, and recognized civil marriage, among other reforms. Tunisia's approach is often considered a model for secularism and gender equality in the region.

In other African countries, the legal systems are often influenced by religious or customary laws that vary depending on the ethnic or religious background of individuals. For instance, countries with a significant Muslim population, such as Egypt, Nigeria, and Sudan, have personal status laws that are influenced by Islamic law (Sharia). These laws can differ from region to region and are applied to individuals who are Muslims. Similarly, countries with a Christian majority may have laws influenced by Christian principles.

The position of a uniform civil code in Africa thus varies across different countries, with some countries implementing aspects of it while others rely on religious or customary laws. The extent of implementation depends on factors such as historical context, cultural diversity, and political considerations.

It should be mentioned that a set of identical laws govern company law in the OHADA region, which covers 17 nations in West and Central Africa. Ten "Uniform Acts" that govern different facets of business activity contain these requirements [29]. The Geneva Convention of 1956 was a major source of inspiration for many of these laws. Until recently, various inter-African conventions and the member states' national laws governed corporation law. The Uniform Act, following the OHADA, is credited for identifying shared regulations throughout the Member States while enhancing legal clarity [30].

- **Position in Middle East**

While the Middle East region is predominantly Muslim and influenced by Islamic law (Sharia), most Middle Eastern countries have specific personal status laws based on their interpretation of Islamic principles. It is important to note that the Middle East is a diverse region with varying legal systems and cultural norms. Therefore, the idea of implementing a uniform civil code in the Middle East faces several challenges due to religious, cultural, and political considerations.

In countries where Islamic law plays a significant role, such as Saudi Arabia, Iran, or Iraq, the implementation of a uniform civil code that deviates from Islamic principles would likely face significant resistance from conservative religious groups and influential religious authorities. These countries have legal systems heavily influenced by Islamic law and have specific personal status laws for different religious communities.

However, it's worth mentioning that some Middle Eastern countries, such as Tunisia, have implemented certain reforms aimed at establishing a more secular legal framework and promoting gender equality. Tunisia's Personal Status Code, for example, provides greater rights and protections for women compared to some other countries in the region.

The implementation of a uniform civil code in the Middle East is a complex and challenging issue due to the region's religious and cultural diversity, as well as the influence of Islamic law in many countries. While some countries have taken steps towards more secular and gender-equitable legal frameworks, the adoption of a comprehensive uniform civil code that overrides religious laws is not widely prevalent in the region [31].

Examining the international perspective on a uniform civil code reveals a diverse range of approaches and considerations. While several countries have implemented a uniform civil code to promote equality and secularism, others have chosen to preserve religious or customary laws for various reasons. The decision to adopt or reject a uniform civil code is often influenced by historical, cultural, and political factors specific to each country.

Proponents of a uniform civil code argue that it fosters social cohesion, gender equality, and individual freedoms by providing a common set of laws for all citizens, regardless of their religious or cultural background. They contend that it promotes a sense of national identity and minimizes discrimination, as everyone is subject to the same legal framework. Uniform civil codes can also simplify legal processes, enhance administrative efficiency, and reduce conflicts arising from conflicting personal laws.

On the other hand, critics express concerns about the potential erosion of cultural and religious diversity, arguing that a uniform civil code may undermine the autonomy and identity of minority communities. They emphasize the importance of protecting and respecting individual rights to religious freedom and cultural practices.

It is important to acknowledge that each country's path toward a uniform civil code is unique and must be shaped by its own social, cultural, and political dynamics. While drawing lessons from international experiences can provide insights and alternative models, it is crucial to tailor any potential implementation to the specific needs and aspirations of the society in question. A thoughtful and inclusive dialogue involving all stakeholders, including religious leaders, legal experts, activists, and citizens, is vital to ensure a comprehensive understanding of the implications and to forge a consensus on the way forward.

To conclude, the implementation of a UCC can bring several benefits that outweigh its cons: and can be seen as a step towards a more progressive and inclusive society. It ensures that all citizens are treated equally before the law, regardless of their religious beliefs. It promotes the principles of justice and fairness by eliminating the disparities and discriminatory practices that may exist under personal laws based on religion. One of the other significant advantages of a UCC is the promotion of gender equality. Personal laws based on religion often contain provisions that discriminate against women in matters such as marriage, divorce, inheritance, and custody of children. A UCC can help eliminate these discriminatory practices and provide equal rights and opportunities to women. It also promotes social cohesion by fostering a sense of common identity and shared values among citizens. It helps bridge the divide created by different personal laws and encourages unity and integration within society. By treating all citizens equally, a UCC can contribute to a more harmonious and inclusive society.

Personal laws based on religion can be complex and difficult to navigate, leading to confusion and legal complications. A uniform civil code simplifies the legal framework by providing a single set of laws that applies to all citizens, making it easier for individuals to understand and access their rights. This simplification can improve access to justice and ensure that everyone is aware of their legal rights and obligations. Finally, a UCC reflects a progressive and modern outlook by emphasizing individual rights and freedoms. It can help address regressive practices and bring personal laws in line with contemporary societal values. By ensuring that laws evolve with the changing times, a UCC can contribute to the overall development and advancement of society.

Simply put, the international perspective on a uniform civil code demonstrates a complex interplay between principles of equality, cultural diversity, and individual freedoms. While some countries have embraced a uniform civil code as a means to promote secularism and gender justice, others have opted for alternative approaches that accommodate religious and cultural plurality. Ultimately, the decision regarding the implementation of a uniform civil code should be undertaken with sensitivity, inclusivity, and a deep understanding of the local context to ensure the protection of individual rights while fostering a just and harmonious society. It is crucial to take into account the diverse cultural and religious beliefs of the citizens and to ensure that the code is inclusive and respects individual rights. Open and inclusive discussions and consultations with all stakeholders are essential to address concerns and ensure a smooth transition towards a uniform civil code.

Notes

1. UCC: Don't look to the West, India has evolved its own way, available at: http://timesofindia.indiatimes.com/articleshow/60507425.cms?utm_source=contentofinterest&utm_medium=text&utm_campaign=cppst (last visited on 15th May, 2023).

2. Id.

3. Uniform Civil Code In Foreign Countries: Its Evaluation From The Perspective Of India, available at: https://legalserviceindia.com/legal/article-7248-uniform-civil-code-in-foreign-countries-its-evaluation-from-the-perspective-of india.html#:~:text=The%20Uniform%20Civil%20Code%20seeks,on%20their%20religion%20or%20ethnicity. (last visited 15th May, 2023).

4. Id.

5. Id.

6. Uniform Acts for Family Law Cases, available at: https://www.dipietropllc.com/blog/2020/january/uniform-acts-for-family-law-cases/ (last visited on 16th May, 2023).

7. Uniform Laws, available at: https://www.law.cornell.edu/uniform#:~:text=Upon%20approval%20by%20the%20National,adopted%20by%20a%20single%20state. (Last visited on 16th May, 2023).

8. Id.

9. Id.

10. Supra Note 4

11. Id.

12. Anirudh Belle, WHEN ETHNIC MINORITIES DIVORCE IN MULTICULTURAL BRITAIN: A SURVEY OF LEGAL CHALLENGES WITH A FOCUS ON THE SOUTH ASIAN EXPERIENCE, (2018) 8 GJLDP (October) 34, available at: http://www.scconline.com (last visited 16th May, 2023).

13. Id.

14. (1972) 2 WLR 347

15. (1974) 118 S.J.

16. (1980) 1 WLR 355

17. Supra note 12

18. (1973) 117 Sol Jo 874.

19. (1973) 117 Sol Jo 582.

20. (1981) 11 Fam Law 110.

21. (1975) 2 WLR 201

22. (1969) 1 WLR 487

23. Supra note 12

24. Id.

25. 14 SASR 1. 19

26. Will India Implement a Uniform Civil Code?, available at: https://www.internationalaffairs.org.au/australianoutlook/will-india-implement-a-uniform-civil-code/ (last visited 17th May, 2017).

27. FEDERALISM AND UNIFORMITY OF LAWS: THE CANADIAN EXPERIENCE, available at: https://scholarship.law.duke.edu/cgi/viewcontent.cgi?article=3055&context=lcp (last visited 17th May, 2023).

28. Id.

29. OHADA's 17 African States Adopt the Uniform Act on Mediation, available at: https://www.jonesday.com/en/insights/2017/12/ohadas-17-african-states-adopt-the-uniform-act-on-mediation (last visited 17th May, 2023).

30. Id.

31. Supra Note 3

CHAPTER 5

Law Commission Recommendations on the Uniform Civil Code

Introduction

The Law Commission of India released a Consultation Paper on Reform of Family Law back in 2018 [1] and there has been radio silence on the government's end after the same. There have been multiple questions that have been raised voicing this concern as to why the government has not said or commented on this issue yet. In 2022, the Centre clarified its position and told the Supreme Court that, there lies a constitutional obligation of upholding the Uniform Civil Code, as India is a diverse country with people from different religions follow their own set of property and marriage laws in order to uphold the national unity of the country. [2] It was further stated by the Centre that, Part IV of the Constitution talks about the

Directive Principles of State Policy and that to the state must ensure that, there is a secure Uniform Civil Code in place all over the country which is exactly what is propounded by Article 44 of the Constitution and is resonating with the preamble of the Constitution as well [3]. Elaborating on the need for the same, the Centre also stated that provision of Article 44 is present so that an integration in brought within India and there is a common platform through which all diverse laws are regulated which are currently regulated by different laws in the country and the need for Article 44 was emphasized on from a social and personal law viewpoint [4]. After the Centre elaborated their stand on the significance that the matter holds, they clarified to the Supreme Court that the matter has been referred to the 22nd Law Commission and that it has been constituted but the examination of various issues and the recommendations for the same are still awaited [5]. It was also categorically noted and highlighted by the center that, this matter was of a legislative nature and that the elected representatives of the people would have a say on the matter and the petition which lies with the Supreme Court should be dismissed with immediate effect. It is extremely important that, the views expressed through the Consultation paper are examined in great detail so as to understand what they say on the matter is and how to further proceed with the same in any kind of manner whatsoever.

Examining the Consultation Paper

In 2016, the Law Commission of India was given the task of examining the issue pertaining to the implementation of the Uniform Civil Code in India and provide their report on it after making heavy deliberations and a detailed analysis of the issue. The Law Commission went ahead and picked up the task to clear out the air of ambiguity that surrounds the subject of the Uniform Civil Code and through the consultation paper an effort was made to understand, acknowledge, and address the issue along with making concrete suggestions which would take into account all the personal laws regulating the citizens of the country. It is extremely important that in performing this task, the secular nature of the country and the diverse population along with their strong views are taken into strict consideration before any solution or perspective is finally provided, so that it does not lead to any discriminatory act taking place which affects any portion of the population and go against the values protected by the Constitution of India.

It was observed that the personal laws which are present in the country are discriminatory towards women and to remove that inequality from the picture, it is immensely important that, certain amendments take place to ensure that there is no ambiguity left in the interpretation of the personal laws and their application on individuals [6]. The question as to whether or not 'personal laws' fall under the ambit of Article 13 of the Constitution or if they are required to be protected under Article 25-28 of the Constitution has been debated multiple times, most notably in the case of State of Bombay v. Narasu Appa Mali [7]. The Commission in their best belief and in the absence of any consensus on the uniform civil code felt that to move forward and preserve the secular state and diversity in the country along with ensuring that personal laws do not superimpose themselves on the fundamental rights guaranteed under the Constitution of India, a very careful recommendation has to be made since this issue at hand is not one which should be taken lightly at all. Therefore, it would be the best way forward to have the family laws and the matters covered thereunder to be codified to the maximum extent possible so that there are no inequalities present in the laws and whichever problematic areas have been identified should be removed by way of these amendments [8].

The Law Commission made a very interesting observation and stated that if any law is to be codified, there is a lot of debate that would go around doing the same and that the act of codification personal laws can be challenged as per Article 14 of the Constitution and therefore, the Commission urged that the legislature shall first ensure that there is equality between men and women and then move on to guarantee equality within communities and this is the way how the differences which are existing within the system will be weeded out and there would be uniformity and equality present at the same time [9]. This one observation is extremely important because if there was to be a uniform civil code in place, it is pertinent that the existing laws have the element of equality present in them after which further changes can be made. There has been a long ongoing war between the right to freedom of religion and right to equality which has made it nearly impossible for any debate on Uniform Civil Code to proceed towards its conclusion and hence, both these rights have to be reconcile and exist in consonance with one another so that there is just administration of law in the country as both these rights are valuable to the citizens and asking to choose one over the other would just put any individual in a problematic position, which is not the aim. The Commission also emphasized on the fact that the secular laws like the Special Marriage Act of 1954 also suffers from various loopholes and that provides an overview to the fact that even these religion neutral laws do not provide any guarantee that there would be justice ensured [10].

These two rights were separately examined as well. On one hand, there is right to freedom of religion and right to practice and propagate religion which has to be protected under the Constitution in a secular democracy which also carries with itself multiple social evils in the name of 'religious customs' such as slavery, sati, triple talaq, inter alia and for their protection within the ambit of religion would be a huge question mark and a grievous mistake as they do not come anywhere near humanity and still continue to exist [11]. Although some religions might consider them as essential in nature, they should not be allowed to continue as that would lead to discrimination in its most raw form [12]. On the other hand, there is right to equality which is again not an absolute right, and it would be a completely grave error to recognize it as an absolute right which can be applied to everyone at the same time because of the very fact that inequality as an essence exist everywhere in our country as a whole [13]. There is no doubt that multiple steps have been consciously taken to recognize the fact that there is a need for affirmative action that would do good to the laws and the ones who are subject to the same and therefore, steps have been taken in that direction in the form of codifying the laws for various communities to bring them on the same page as the other.

The category of personal laws mostly evolved during the British colonial era and has continued to develop till date [14]. One of the most notable legislations concerned itself with the amendment of the Hindu laws and legislations despite the oppositions from various religious groups which was a bold move on part of the legislature in order to bring the laws on a level which is not only equitable but is also treating every person in the same manner [15]. Dr. B.R. Ambedkar through his views expressed in the constituent assembly debates have also stated that such a uniform civil code is although desirable but should remain voluntary as it would ultimately be the decision of the citizens as to which law would they be governed by as per the Constitution of India and that fact should be respected at all times [16]. The Law Commission had also put forth a questionnaire for the public's opinion in November 2016 through which they wanted to find out whether there should be legal reform brought in or not and they received many responses through which they figured that there are some issues which needed immediate attention and the most pertinent one was triple talaq that needed special attention [17]. Therefore, keeping in mind India's diversity, secularism and other factors, the Commission proceeded ahead for dealing with discriminatory laws rather than providing for a uniform civil code, which they thought would be a step in the right direction that they would be initiating.

Recommendations of the Consultation Paper

The Law Panel through their Consultation Paper did take an open stand in favor of equality within communities, as discussed in detail in the above section. Initially, the intent of the Consultation Paper was to examine the issue of having a Uniform Civil Code to have the best personal laws codified and applicable to all citizens, but the debate came down to limitation of provisions of personal laws of certain communities and removing those provisions which perpetuated inequality amongst citizens and ensuring that there is no inequality between individuals before jumping onto the communities [18]. Currently, the Indian Constitution allows various communities to follow their own personal laws with regard to marriage, divorce, inheritance, succession, inter alia which is provided for under Article 25, whereas Article 44 which speaks about a Uniform Civil Code is only a directive principle of state policy and is not mandated in any manner.

The Law Panel through its Consultation Paper carved out various criticisms which were against the implementation of the Uniform Civil Code and some of them were that they saw the UCC as an interfering tool on most of the personal laws of the minorities of the country, they also noted that a UCC will infringe on one of the fundamental rights of the minorities which has been provided under Article 25 which cannot be stepped on as per the Constitution [19]. It was further noted that, in a diverse country like India where so many communities and religious groups and cultures exist, it would be a near impossible task to implement such a UCC and have positive results streaming out of it, as there would not only be social debates associated with its implementation but also political debates that will crop up during the elections which would not be the best bet to place as the thoughts of one party and the other party don't need to be in alignment with each other and that would eventually create a havoc in the country which is not desirable [20]. Lastly, the very fact which was stated was that this implementation of a UCC will be against the values that a secular state should hold in the first place which are not being regarded and respected and therefore, a certain bunch of people cannot have the decision-making power as to which laws will be applicable to individuals all around the country whether or not it is their independent choice or not [21]. Therefore, looking at the criticism which were pointed out by the Panel, it can be safe to conclude that there was not much favor inclined towards having a UCC in place in the country and the Panel gave multiple reasons for supporting their ideology for the same which have already been noted. However, the Law Panel was completely in favor of amending and codifying the personal laws that suffer due to the presence of the element of inequality and which require a necessary amendment to take place.

The Law Panel went ahead and made certain recommendations that are noteworthy and are as follows:

1. Treatment of a Muslim women equivalent to that of a father in the capacity of a natural guardian [22]. Although, this recommendation is in the right direction, the implementation in practice is extremely difficult to achieve and if this were to take place as a part of a Uniform Civil Code, the uniformity would be much more visible.

2. Enactment of a legislation which would make the birth of a child born out of a live-in relationship legitimate along with having various rights including inheritance [23]. This was a very interesting recommendation which was very progressive in the right direction. However, the acceptance into every religion of the same and their personal laws is debatable

and hence, a Uniform Civil Code is much more preferable to ensure that such a recommendation when executed is followed.

3. Creating an equal age for marriage which is 18 years for both boys and girls, which basically meant bringing down the marriage age for boys from 21 years [24]. Although this step might be applauded by many, the critique here is to bring the age of both the genders to 21 years of age and ensuring that all personal laws follow the same, however, because of the existing differences this would be extremely unlikely unless there is a Unified Code.

4. Simplification of divorce proceedings so as to encourage individuals for not bringing in false cases and to ensure a smooth exit for both parties [25]. This was done to stop false proceedings from taking place, however, the best way for simplification is to have a Code which applies to all religions equally and the process is streamlined.

5. Amendment of the Special Marriage Act and ensure that a 30 days' notice is provided to the registrar and there is no misuse by families in case of inter-religious or inter-caste marriages [26]. This was done in the interest of the parties who avail this Act in order to marry out of their

cast and religion and ensure that they are protected in every manner.

6. Ensuring that polygamy is a crime in all communities along with giving out a clarification in the Nikah Halala itself [27]. This recommendation was brought in so that there is the element of equality within the law the continues to be maintained and that there is no unfair treatment provided to one gender while the other is kept on a higher pedestal. However, since the Muslim personal law has been expressly spelled out, this will cause chaos and therefore, codifying the personal laws and prohibiting polygamy would be more efficient.

The above mentioned are only some of the recommendations which the Law Panel wanted to bring into the personal laws that exist within the country to ensure that there is no inequality and that every individual has their guaranteed rights protected to exercise them whenever they want to without any fear and with the backing of the law which is in line with their religion as well. However, having critiqued the laws, it can only be said that the better option is codification of these laws into a Uniform Civil Code which will end the evils that are still persisting.

Conclusion

As a conclusion remark and a way forward in the debate it can be stated that the reforms that have been brought in are to ensure that the laws are contemporary, progressive and gender neutral in nature to keep up with the changing times [28]. When it comes to the implementation of a Uniform Civil Code, it would be a practice through which there would a combination exercise where all the laws and best practices from all religions are picked and a central code for reference is created, which also will lead to building trust between the various communities, as per the Law Panel [29]. The nature of development in the jurisprudence on the essential practices doctrine as mentioned above, indicates an attempt by the Indian state to promote a set of principles that can be viewed as integral to all religions and thus seeks to set a common standard to measure the essentiality of various religious practices. India does not have a separate legislation on human rights. The values of human rights have been imbibed into the constitutional legal order [31]. However, the implementation part of the UCC is the biggest evil that is surrounding it since the time it has come into discussions and implementation is affected by various factors at a huge level, one of them being political and social environments which will have varying views as to whether a UCC is desirable or not. There have been brilliant arguments which have been put forth both for and against the UCC since the very beginning of the colonial era up until today. Recognizing both the sides and the observations which have been given by the Law Panel through their consultation paper as well, it would be safe to state and assume that they believe that a UCC is not desirable and would not have a positive effect in the society for which it is being implemented and since, it is likely to fail at achieving the desired goals, there lies no point in performing such an act which is bound to be futile and have nothing improved as an end result of the same. However, if the points of the Law Panel are to be considered from an implementation perspective, codification and uniformity through a UCC would be the most ideal way to achieve the same and hence the author argues that the implementation of UCC should be weighed on a higher pedestal. The secular state argument and the right to religion does not need to be eliminated to bring a UCC in action as India will still continue to be secular and home to multiple diverse communities who will be governed by one codified law but will be allowed to follow their religion and practices associated with the same. Therefore, it is the need of the hour to bring such a code in place to fight the known devil and be prepared for any unknown enemies which might affect the diversity of India.

Notes

1. *Explained: Uniform Civil Code And Centre's Reference To 22nd Law Commission,* Outlook (Feb.19, 2023), https://www.outlookindia.com/national/explained-uniform-civil-code-centre-to-refer-matters-to-the-22nd-law-commission-news-231010

2. *Id.*

3. *Id.*

4. *Id.*

5. *Id.*

6. Law Commission of India, Consultation Paper on Reform of Family Law (2018), https://images.assettype.com/barandbench/import/2018/08/Consultation-Paper-LCI-Family-Law.pdf

7. *Id.*

8. *Id.*

9. *Id.*

10. *Id.*

11. *Id.*

12. *Id.*

13. *Id.*

14. *Id.*

15. *Id.*

16. *Id.*

17. *Id.*

18. *Law Commission on Uniform Civil Code In India,* Chronicle (Feb. 24, 2023),

https://www.chronicleindia.in/articles/47-law-commission-on-uniform-civil-code-in-india

19. *Id.*

20. *Id.*

21. *Id.*

22. *Id.*

23. *Id.*

24. *Id.*

25. *Id.*

26. *Id.*

27. *Id.*

28. *Id.*

29. *Id.*

30. Joseph Minattur, *The Story of a Civil Code,* JILI 150-152 (1976)

31. Kalindi Kokal, *Uniformity in Diversity? Reflecting on the Essential Practices Doctrine and its Implications for Legal Pluralism,* NSLR 18-23 (2020)

32. Brijraj Deora, *Special Marriage Act (1954) as a precursor of uniform civil code,* CNLULJ 235-238, (2020)

CHAPTER 6

UCC Is Not An Anti-Thesis To Religion

India is a country that is often described as a melting pot of cultures and religions. With a population of over 1.3 billion people, India is home to people from diverse religious, cultural, and linguistic backgrounds. While considering the debate of Uniform Civil Code and its implementation in India, religion and its vast variety is considered to be one of the most crucial roadblocks. The implementation of a Uniform Civil Code in India has been a subject of debate and controversy for several decades, with religious groups often playing a significant role in shaping the discussion and determining the outcome. The idea of Uniform Civil Code has been envisaged in the Indian Constitution under Article 44 of the Directive Principles of State Policy, which states that the State shall endeavour to secure for the citizens a uniform civil code throughout the territory of India. The objective of the Uniform Civil Code is to bring about unity and cohesion among different communities, promote gender equality, social justice, and national integration. The Uniform Civil Code proposes to create a common civil law for all citizens that would be based on principles of justice, equity, and fair play.

The problem which comes up while trying to introduce such unity and cohesion is the regard each religious community has for their own religious practices and customs which is fair enough and is protected under Article 25 of Constitution of India. It is imperative for us to understand that the intent of Uniform Civil Code is not erosion of these practices but instead bring all "essential" customs together in a manner which is beneficial to all. At the end of the day, we must let go of such religious practices which are detrimental to us as a society at large. We have to learn to welcome practices which bring us all together, unify us and in turn help us erode the bitterness between religious groups. The very intent of Uniform Civil Code is this- integration of the nation as a whole.

It is but obvious that before our grand Uniform Civil Code can do their magic, we need to do our homework. We need to understand the ground realities with which we would be working upon while trying to bring the country under one code for civil laws, in particular. It is for such intents and purposes that it is important to at the foremost understand the religious demographics of the country, post which we would delve into the impact of various religious groups on the prospects for a Uniform Civil Code in India. While we would be reading into the thought process each religious group has had over the implementation of Uniform Civil Code in India, we would be understanding the laws which govern the personal affairs. In order to holistically understand the entire picture with respect to the Uniform Civil Code and its interaction with religion.

Religious Demography of India

We know and tend to acknowledge it with immense pride that India is a land of diverse religious beliefs and practices. We are home to several major religions and numerous smaller ones which are coexisting in the country. Religion has been an integral part of Indian society and culture for centuries, and the country has a rich and complex religious history. This is why it is pertinent that we explore the religious demographics of India, including the major religions, their distribution, and their historical and cultural significance.

Hinduism is the largest religion in India, with over 1 billion adherents, making up more than three fourths of the population of our country. It is also one of the world's oldest religions, with its roots dating back to ancient India. Hinduism is a polytheistic religion, with a wide variety of gods and goddesses worshipped by its followers. The religion has many rituals, practices, and beliefs, and is closely tied to Indian culture and traditions. [1]

Islam is the second-largest religion in India, with over 200 million adherents, making up around a sixth of the country's population. Islam was introduced to India in the 7th century, and has had a significant impact on Indian society and culture. Muslims in India are mainly concentrated in the northern and western regions of the country, with large populations in states such as Uttar Pradesh, Bihar, and West Bengal. [2]

Christianity is the third-largest religion in India, with over 28 million adherents, making up around two per cent of the country's population- which in per cent may seem less but is significant in quantam. Christianity was introduced to India by the Apostle Thomas in the 1st century and has since spread to different parts of the country. Christians in India are mainly concentrated in the southern states of Kerala, Tamil Nadu, and Goa. [3]

Sikhism is a religion that originated in India in the 15th century, and has around 27 million adherents, making up around 2% of the country's population. Sikhism is monotheistic, and its follower's worship one God, known as Waheguru. The religion has its origins in the Punjab region of India and is closely tied to Punjabi culture and traditions. [4]

Buddhism is a religion that originated in India in the 6th century BC, and has around 8 million adherents, making up less than 1% of the country's population. Buddhism has had a significant impact on Indian history and culture, and its teachings have influenced many other religions and philosophies around the world. Buddhists in India are mainly concentrated in the northern and eastern regions of the country. [5]

Jainism is a religion that originated in India in the 6th century BC, and has around 5 million adherents, making up less than a per cent of the population of the country. Jainism is a religion that emphasizes non-violence and self-control, and its followers are mainly concentrated in the western regions of India. [6]

In addition to these major religions, India is also home to several smaller religions and indigenous faiths, including Zoroastrianism, Judaism, and Baha'i. These religions have relatively small numbers of adherents in India but have had a significant impact on the country's religious and cultural diversity. [7]

Now the fun part is that indeed, there have been challenges and tensions with respect to the diversity in religion in India, however at the same time, our country has a beautiful history of religious tolerance and coexistence. There are instances of tensions between religious groups but at the same time, there are several instances of love between the two groups. It is undeniable that our country's secular constitution enshrines the principle of religious freedom and prohibits discrimination on the basis of religion. This is primarily the reason why something like Uniform Civil Code will never be able to sow discord, it would instead help in reducing the distance between the various religious groups.

That being said we cannot also deny that there is still work to be done to promote greater understanding and harmony between different religious communities in India, and to address the underlying causes of religious conflicts and tensions. With continued efforts towards interfaith dialogue and understanding, India can continue to build a more peaceful and inclusive society, one that celebrates the diversity of its religious traditions and cultures.

If we look at such efforts, there are numerous. In recent years, the Indian government has taken steps to promote interfaith harmony and understanding. In 2010, the Ministry of Home Affairs established the National Foundation for Communal Harmony (NFCH) to provide assistance and support to victims of communal violence and to promote interfaith dialogue and understanding. The government has also established several other initiatives and programs aimed at promoting communal harmony, including the Prime Minister's 15 Point Programme for Minorities and the National Integration Council.[8]

In addition to government initiatives, there are also many civil society organizations and groups working to promote interfaith dialogue and understanding in India. These include organizations like the Interfaith Harmony Foundation, the Interfaith Coalition for Peace, and the Interfaith Youth Network, which bring together people from different religious backgrounds to promote understanding and cooperation.

Despite these efforts, however, there is still much work to be done to address the underlying causes of religious conflict and tension in India. Some of the key factors that contribute to religious tensions in the country include economic inequality, political polarization, and the rise of extremist groups and ideologies. Such challenges need to be acknowledged and addressed so that we nip it all in the bud. Otherwise, problems like economic inequality can lead to resentment and tensions between different religious communities, particularly when one community is seen as having greater economic power and privilege. Political polarization can fuel tensions and conflicts between different communities, particularly during elections and other political events. [9]

Addressing these underlying factors will require a concerted effort from all segments of Indian society, including the government, civil society organizations, and religious leaders. It will require a commitment to promoting greater understanding and cooperation between different religious communities, as well as addressing the economic and political factors that contribute to religious tensions. The introduction of Uniform Civil Code, which is believed to be one of the highlights in the manifesto of the current ruling party in the upcoming elections of 2024, does present a viable solution. [10]

The stance of various religious communities in India regarding the implementation of a Uniform Civil Code is intricate and diverse. Although certain groups are staunch advocates of a Uniform Civil Code, there are also numerous groups that harbor apprehensions and reservations regarding its potential effects on their respective religious customs and rituals. We must understand that discussion of a Uniform Civil Code in India will need to take into account the views and concerns of all religious groups and will require a delicate balance between promoting secularism and protecting the rights of religious minorities.

We cannot avoid all the issues which exist within the current set up in India. We cannot not acknowledge that we are home to a vast number of religious groups- each of them holding their own practices dear. At the same time, we cannot and must not shy away from such reforms which can help us be a unified country and Uniform Civil Code might just be the solution for it. Discussions around it are imperative since it is them which allow us to identify the issues and loopholes and walk towards a better future. Uniform Civil Code is not here to subsume any religion nor is it there to take away our right to religion, it is merely there to do away with the bad of one religion, adopt the good of the same and bring all religions under one civil code. It is as simple as that.

Personal Laws in India

Article 25 of the Constitution of India, the clause (1) of which reads as "*Subject to public order, morality and health and to the other provisions of this Part, all persons are equally entitled to freedom of conscience and the right freely to profess, practise and propagate religion.".* Article 25 of the Indian Constitution guarantees the freedom of religion to all citizens, which includes the right to profess, practice, and propagate one's own religion. This has been interpreted to mean that individuals and communities have the right to follow their own personal laws and customs in matters of marriage, divorce, and inheritance, among other things.

Personal laws in India refer to the legal systems that apply to specific religious communities in matters such as marriage, divorce, and inheritance. These laws are based on religious texts, customs, and traditions, and are recognized and enforced by the Indian legal system. Such set of laws apply to several religious communities in India, including Hindus, Muslims, Christians, Parsis, and Jews. Each religious community has its own personal laws, which may differ significantly from those of other communities. However, as political scientist Asim Ali has opined, the *"reality is more complex"*.

Hindu personal laws govern marriage and divorce for Hindus and are based on the Hindu Marriage Act of 1955 and the Hindu Succession Act of 1956. These laws govern issues such as the minimum age of marriage, the validity and grounds for divorce, and the distribution of property after death. Muslim personal laws, on the other hand, are based on the Quran and the Hadith, and are governed by the Muslim Personal Law (Shariat) Application Act of 1937. These laws govern issues such as the validity and grounds for marriage and divorce, as well as inheritance and property rights. [11]

Christian personal laws are based on the Indian Christian Marriage Act of 1872 and the Indian Succession Act of 1925. These laws govern issues such as the validity and grounds for marriage and divorce, as well as inheritance and property rights. Parsi personal laws are based on the Parsi Marriage and Divorce Act of 1936 and the Parsi Succession Act of 1925. [12] These laws govern issues such as the validity and grounds for marriage and divorce, as well as inheritance and property rights. Jewish personal laws are based on Jewish religious texts and traditions, and are recognized by the Indian legal system. These laws govern issues such as marriage and divorce, as well as inheritance and property rights.

Personal laws have been a subject of controversy and debate in India, with many arguing that they are discriminatory and perpetuate inequality and injustice. It is such basis such line of thought that there have been several calls for a Uniform Civil Code that would apply to all citizens of India, regardless of their religion, and would help to promote equality and secularism. As always, some haters assume that Uniform Civil Code would merely subsume religion and its practices within itself. It is opined by them that personal laws are an important part of religious identity and should be protected. At the end of the day, as mentioned earlier, the debate over personal laws in India is complex and multifaceted. In a country of the size of India, any potential changes will need to take into account the views and concerns of all religious communities in the country and there would be haters in every scenario.

Personal laws have been an integral component of India's legal system for a significant period of time. However, there has been growing concern over their effect on women and underprivileged communities. Detractors claim that personal laws frequently display gender bias and reinforce patriarchal beliefs, particularly with regards to marriage, divorce, and inheritance. Lately, there have been calls for reforms to personal laws. The interpretation of Article 25 has been a central issue in this debate. Some argue that Article 25 protects the right of individuals and communities to follow their own personal laws and customs, while others argue that it should not be used to justify discrimination and inequality.

In recent years, this alarmingly increasing scrutiny of personal laws in India, particularly in relation to the treatment of women must be duly noted. Critics argue that personal laws often discriminate against women and perpetuate patriarchal values, particularly in matters of marriage, divorce, and inheritance. For example, under Muslim personal laws, a man can divorce his wife by pronouncing "talaq" three times, while a woman does not have the same right. This practice, known as "triple talaq", has been widely criticized for being discriminatory and violating women's rights. In 2017, the Indian government passed a law banning triple talaq, but the issue remains controversial.

Similarly, under Hindu personal laws, women have historically had limited rights in matters of inheritance. While the Hindu Succession Act of 1956 did provide some reforms, such as giving daughters equal rights to inherit ancestral property, there are still many gaps and ambiguities in the law that make it difficult for women to exercise their rights.

At the time of independence, the Constitution of India largely preserved the "Hindu" and "Mohammedan" laws. Consequently, the personal laws in existence today are primarily based on customs that were favorable to the indigenous patriarchy. Building on this argument, Nalini Rajan examined two landmark cases where personal laws were challenged in court - Rakhmabai (involving a Hindu woman) [13] and Shah Bano (involving a Muslim woman) [14] - and concluded that reforming personal laws may not be feasible unless driven by women due to the entwined nature of religion and patriarchy.[15] Even after Hindu Personal Law abolished polygamy post-independence, there was a violent public uproar where Hindu men threatened to convert to Islam as they felt that their "customary rights" were being taken away.

The debate over personal laws in India is closely tied to the debate over a Uniform Civil Code. Supporters of a Uniform Civil Code argue that it would help to promote equality and secularism and would remove the discrimination and inequality that are inherent in personal laws. However, opponents argue that a Uniform Civil Code would be an imposition of Hindu values on other religious communities, and could lead to the loss of autonomy and identity for minority groups. [16]

In recent years, there have been some attempts to reform personal laws in India without introducing a Uniform Civil Code. For example, the Indian government has passed several laws to protect the rights of women, such as the Protection of Women from Domestic Violence Act of 2005 and the Sexual Harassment of Women at Workplace (Prevention, Prohibition and Redressal) Act of 2013. There have also been some efforts to modernize personal laws within religious communities. For example, some Muslim scholars have called for reforms to the Muslim personal law to address issues such as gender equality, child marriage, and divorce. [17] Similarly, some Hindu groups have called for reforms to Hindu personal laws to address issues such as inheritance and property rights for women. However, at the end of the day it all boils down to one thing- an imminent need to bring all the personal laws under one civil code which could allow for the betterment of the country as a whole.

Goa: Sample Case for Uniform Civil Code

While discussing Uniform Civil Code and religion, we would be amiss if we ignore Goa, the union territory which has pioneered in implementing such Code which lies at the heart of countless political and academic debates. There are countless lessons which we can carry over while we seek to implement the same largely to rest of the nation. To understand the same in depth, we must understand the demographics and the likes of it of the Union Territory.

The union territory is a unique case in India where a Uniform Civil Code has been implemented for several decades. The territory of Goa was a Portuguese colony until 1961, and during this time, a civil code based on Portuguese law was introduced that applied equally to all citizens, regardless of religion. After Goa became a part of India, the Portuguese Civil Code was replaced with the Indian Civil Code. However, Goa retained its unique civil code, known as the Goa Civil Code or the Goa Family Law, which applies equally to all residents of the state, regardless of their religion. [18]

The Goa Civil Code is a Uniform Civil Code in that it provides a common set of laws for marriage, divorce, and inheritance, among other things. The code is based on the principles of equality and non-discrimination and includes provisions that ensure the equal rights of men and women in matters of inheritance, property rights, and divorce. The Goa Civil Code covers a range of personal laws, including those related to marriage, divorce, adoption, inheritance, and property rights. It also includes provisions for child custody and maintenance and recognizes the rights of women to hold property and assets in their own name. [19]

One of the key features of the Goa Civil Code is its emphasis on individual rights and autonomy, rather than community identity. Under the code, individuals have the right to choose their own marriage partners and to dissolve their marriages if they wish, without the need for community or religious approval. [20] This is important from the perspective of religion in particular. By removing the "religious approval" from the quotient, we bypass the issues which crop up when we talk of religion and Uniform Civil Code. Such lesson is pertinent to be taken into account.

Another one of the key features of the Goa Civil Code is that it recognizes the concept of community property, which means that all property acquired during a marriage is jointly owned by both spouses, regardless of who purchased it or whose name is on the title. This provision is aimed at promoting gender equality, and ensuring that women have an equal share in marital assets. Herein, what is important for us is the sense of community which Goa Civil Code lent and which the Uniform Civil Code yearns for. The sense of community which the uniformity can bring about is impeccable and important for unification of the country as a whole.

Another important aspect of the Goa Civil Code is that it provides for equal rights of inheritance for both sons and daughters. This is a departure from traditional Hindu personal law, which gives preference to male heirs in matters of inheritance. The provision for equal inheritance rights for daughters has been hailed as a significant step towards promoting gender equality in the state. Such bold choice of departure from the traditional personal laws and yet emerging to be successful is something which we as a country seek to adopt. The choice here is whether we choose to let go of the old system of patriarchal norms and thinking, working towards a better future or, do we maintain our faith in our religion and not move forward.

The Goa Civil Code is seen as a progressive and inclusive legal framework that promotes gender equality and individual rights, while also respecting the diversity of Goa's religious communities. The code has been credited with reducing gender-based violence and discrimination and providing greater legal protections for women. Such serves as a prime example for rest of the country and marks our goals for the implementation of the Uniform Civil Code.

It is not that the implementation of the Goa Civil Code has not been without its challenges. Like the Uniform Civil Code, it has also faced criticism from some quarters who argued at that juncture that it violates their constitutional rights. Some groups have raised concerns that the code violates their right to follow their own personal laws and customs, and that it is an imposition of Western values on Indian society. Despite these criticisms, the Goa Civil Code has been in place for several decades and has served as an example of how a Uniform Civil Code can work in practice. While there are undoubtedly challenges in implementing a Uniform Civil Code at the national level, the experience of Goa suggests that it is possible to create a common set of laws that applies equally to all citizens, regardless of religion.

The example of Goa also suggests that a Uniform Civil Code can help to promote gender equality and individual rights, while also respecting the diversity of India's religious communities. While there may be challenges in implementing such a code, the benefits in terms of promoting equality and non-discrimination are clear. It is such benefits which we must look towards and not think that our right to religion is violated.

We must remember that the implementation of a Uniform Civil Code aims to remove the negative aspects of our religion and promote the adoption of better practices from other religions, rather than violating our right to practice religion. This will lead to a convergence of different practices under a single banner. By providing a common set of laws that applies to all citizens, regardless of their religion, the code would help to create a sense of shared identity and community, as it did among the diverse population of Goa.

The Goa Civil Code is indeed based on the principles of equality and non-discrimination and provides a common framework which could help to reduce the influence of communalism and sectarianism. It must be noted that the code has been in place for several decades, and that there has been no significant opposition or agitation for its repeal. Such factors again are imperative as lessons for the implementation of Uniform Civil Code.

The case of Goa illustrates the potential benefits of a Uniform Civil Code for promoting gender equality, individual rights, and social harmony. While there are undoubtedly challenges in implementing such a code at the national level, the example of Goa provides a useful model for how a common set of laws can be developed that applies equally to all citizens, regardless of religion. Whether or not a Uniform Civil Code is ultimately adopted at the national level, the experience of Goa provides important lessons for how personal laws can be reformed to promote greater equality and social justice.

A Balancing Act

Our present discussion herein is grounded on religion because a fear exists in our minds that bringing uniformity in our religion, in our culture would erode away our identity and that it would in turn take away from us our right to religion. However, we forget that this religion we talk of is not uniform in itself and that all parts of it are not our identity. For instance, the Hindu Code, which aimed to establish a uniform law for all Hindus, is not entirely uniform when it comes to essential aspects. For example, the validity of a marriage is linked to the customs and ceremonies of a particular community. Additionally, inheritance rights and rules on adoption vary between communities in different regions, and the Hindu Minority and Guardianship Act, 1956 does not automatically apply to members of Scheduled Tribes.

The Indian judiciary has played a significant role in balancing the right to practice religion with the need for a Uniform Civil Code. In various cases, the courts have upheld the right to freedom of religion while also calling for a common civil code to promote equality and social justice. For example, in the landmark case of Shah Bano v. Mohammad Ahmed Khan [21], the Supreme Court upheld the right of a Muslim woman to maintenance under the Indian Penal Code, despite opposition from some Muslim groups who argued that it violated Islamic law. The court held that fundamental rights guaranteed by the Constitution could not be overridden by personal laws based on religion.

Similarly, in Sarla Mudgal v. Union of India [22], the Supreme Court held that a Hindu husband's conversion to Islam solely to practice polygamy was illegal and violated the principles of equality and non-discrimination. The court emphasized the need for a Uniform Civil Code to ensure uniformity and promote social cohesion.

The need for a Uniform Civil Code was also highlighted in the case of Ms. Jorden Diengdeh v. S.S. Chopra [23]. The court emphasized that marriage-related laws, such as judicial separation and divorce, are not uniform in India, and thus, the need for a uniform marriage-related law, such as irreversible dissolution of marriage and mutual consent for divorce, is crucial irrespective of religion. The court stressed the need for a Uniform Civil Code for marriage and divorce and directed the Ministry of Law and Justice to implement its judgment.

However, the implementation of a Uniform Civil Code has been a contentious issue, with various groups expressing concerns over its potential impact on religious and cultural practices. Some argue that a uniform code would undermine the diversity of India's cultural and religious traditions, while others contend that it would lead to a more just and equitable society. In response to these concerns, the judiciary has emphasized that any implementation of a Uniform Civil Code should be done with sensitivity and caution, taking into account the diversity of India's cultural and religious traditions. The courts have also called for dialogue and consultation with various stakeholders, including religious and community leaders, to ensure that any reforms are implemented in a manner that respects the rights and beliefs of all citizens.

Further, if we deep dive more into the issue of conflict with Article 25, we must circle back to the root of what the constitution makers seek to bring out by way of Article 25. Article 25 of India's Constitution provides religious freedom. This means that all citizens have the freedom to freely practise their religion, free from government intervention. However, Article 25 specifies that this liberty is not absolute. The government has the authority to limit religious freedom in order to maintain other basic rights, such as the right to equality. The Uniform Civil Code does not violate Article 25 since it does not hinder religious freedom. The Uniform Civil Code would not forbid anyone from freely practising their religion. It would merely ensure that all people, regardless of religion, are treated equally under the law.

The adoption of a Uniform Civil Code would go on to alleviate the problem of discrimination and inequality in personal law. Many personal laws are biased against specific groups of people, notably women, and perpetuate inequities based on religious beliefs. A Uniform Civil Code would assure the protection of fundamental rights, particularly the right to equality, by establishing a single civil code that treats all people equally. This is consistent with Article 25 since it promotes equality and protects persons from discrimination.

Thereby at the end of the day whether the Uniform Civil Code would be able to balance the constitutional mandate and the religious freedoms of people would all depend on its implementation. It would ultimately be a balancing act.

Uniform Civil Code: Viable Solution for Religious Discord

Uniform Civil Code can be an effective tool to resolve religious discord in India by promoting a sense of equality and justice among all citizens, regardless of their religion. With a Uniform Civil Code, personal laws of various religions can be replaced by a common set of laws, which will ensure that all individuals are treated equally in matters such as marriage, divorce, inheritance, and property rights and at the same time our right to religion under Article 25 remains wholly intact.

By having a common set of laws, Uniform Civil Code can promote a sense of unity among different religions and help in reducing religious tensions. By promoting a common understanding of legal rights and obligations, a Uniform Civil Code can help to foster a sense of national identity and promote a shared sense of citizenship.

It can also promote gender equality by ensuring that women are treated equally under the law, irrespective of their religion. Implementing a Uniform Civil Code in India has the potential to promote religious harmony and reduce communal tensions by creating a shared legal framework for all citizens, regardless of their religion. It can also help to eliminate discriminatory laws and practices that are prevalent in personal laws based on religion. This would not only bring about greater gender equality, but also create a sense of unity and social cohesion by promoting a common national identity.

Furthermore, implementing a Uniform Civil Code would signal the government's commitment to secularism and a clear separation of religion and state [24]. It would also demonstrate that the state is not biased towards any particular religion and is committed to ensuring equal treatment for all citizens. It is important to note that Uniform Civil Code should not be seen as an attack on any particular religion or community. It should be implemented through a process of dialogue and consensus-building among all stakeholders, including religious leaders and communities. This will help in creating a sense of ownership and acceptance of the Uniform Civil Code among all communities.

It is important to ensure that the implementation of a Uniform Civil Code in India is done in a manner that respects the country's diverse religious and cultural traditions. This can be achieved by carefully considering the perspectives and apprehensions of all communities while formulating the code, and by implementing it in a gradual and phased manner to allow for a smooth transition.

The Constitution of India was designed to bring together and integrate the diverse religious beliefs of its citizens, but unfortunately, it could not fully achieve this goal. Although the guiding principles of the Indian Constitution acknowledge diversity, they also seek to promote uniformity among people of different faiths. It is for this very reason that we need Uniform Civil Code. It was ultimately this what our constitution called for- unity in diversity and it is not that by bringing uniformity that we dispose of the diversity but instead we learn to arrange our diverse coins in a manner that a uniform set of laws are applicable to them.

Supporters of the Uniform Civil Code argue that it would simplify the complex laws relating to marriage, inheritance, succession, and adoption and make them easier for all to understand and apply. The Uniform Civil Code would also unify India's personal laws, which are currently divided based on religious values and customs. India has various sets of personal laws, such as Hindu personal laws, Shariat law, Parsi law, Christian law, etc. Therefore, a uniform set of personal laws is highly desirable for India's unity and dignity. [25]

However, its implementation is highly controversial and debatable because religious minorities oppose it. Opponents of the Uniform Civil Code argue that personal laws are derived from religious values and should not be interfered with as this might lead to hostility and friction between different religious groups. To this, we must understand that it is not that Uniform Civil Code will bring hostility but instead it will end hostility and lead India to a better and brighter future.

Those challenging the Uniform Civil Code in India also argue that India is a secular republic and freedom of religion is a fundamental right. Furthermore, Articles 29 and 30 guarantee minorities the right to practice their own faith, culture, and customs. Therefore, implementation of the Uniform Civil Code in India would be difficult. Undoubtedly, a strong political will, along with a sense of tolerance for other religions and mutual respect for each other, is required for the implementation of the Uniform Civil Code.

The debate over whether India should replace its current religious personal law system with a Uniform Civil Code has spurred discussions on national integration, modernity, secularism, and gender equality. The current personal law system is seen as problematic from an equality perspective as it provides different laws for members of different religious communities and treats men and women unequally. Introducing a secular Uniform Civil Code could potentially solve these issues. However, there is a global trend towards recognizing "normative orderings beyond the state's reach" and acknowledging that many people in the developing world use informal or non-state legal systems.

At the end of it all, we must remember that it is not that our right to religion is violated, instead it is that the bad parts of our religion are being removed, paving way for adoption of better practices in other religions- all culminating under one banner of Uniform Civil Code. We cannot ignore the issues that currently exist in India, including the vast number of religious groups and their respective practices. However, we must also acknowledge the potential benefits of reforms that can help unify the country, such as the implementation of a Uniform Civil Code. Discussions surrounding this topic are crucial as they allow us to identify issues and shortcomings and move towards a better future.

It is important to note that a Uniform Civil Code is not intended to undermine or overshadow any religion, but rather to eliminate the negative aspects of personal laws and adopt positive elements from various religions, resulting in a unified civil code for all citizens. The goal is to simplify the legal system and promote equality and justice for all. While it is important to respect and acknowledge the diversity of India's religious groups, we must also recognize the potential benefits of a Uniform Civil Code in promoting unity and justice. Open discussions about the topic are necessary to identify concerns and work towards a brighter future for all citizens.

Notes

1. Stephanie Kramer, "Religious Composition of India", Pew Research Center, September 21, 2021.

2. Id.

3. Id.

4. Id.

5. Id.

6. Id.

7. Id.

8. National Foundation for Communal Harmony, https://nfch.nic.in/.

9. Sahoo, Niranjan. "MOUNTING MAJORITARIANISM AND POLITICAL POLARIZATION IN INDIA." Political Polarization in South and Southeast Asia: Old Divisions, New Dangers, edited by Thomas Carothers and Andrew O'Donohue, Carnegie Endowment for International Peace, 2020, pp. 9–24. JSTOR.

10. IANS, "BJP to give big push to UCC plans ahead of 2024 elections", Deccan Herald, Dec 11, 2022.

11. Subramanian, Narendra. Nation and Family: Personal Law, Cultural Pluralism, and Gendered Citizenship in India. 1st ed., Stanford University Press, 2014. JSTOR.

12. NEWBIGIN, ELEANOR. "Personal Law and Citizenship in India's Transition to Independence." Modern Asian Studies, vol. 45, no. 1, 2011, pp. 7–32. JSTOR.

13. Bhikaji vs. Rukhmabai, 1885

14. Mohd. Ahmad Khan v. Shah Bano Begum [1985 (1) SCALE 767

15. EPW Engage, "Personal Laws versus Gender Justice: Will a Uniform Civil Code Solve the Problem?", 1 Nov 2018.

16. Rattan, Jyoti. "UNIFORM CIVIL CODE IN INDIA: A BINDING OBLIGATION UNDER INTERNATIONAL AND DOMESTIC LAW." Journal of the Indian Law Institute, vol. 46, no. 4, 2004, pp. 577-87. JSTOR

17. Javed Anand, "Time for a serious introspection and reform", The Hindu, August 22, 2017.

18. DESOUZA, PETER RONALD. "Politics of the Uniform Civil Code in India." Economic and Political Weekly, vol. 50, no. 48, 2015, pp. 50-57. JSTOR.

19. Paul, Sandip, "Uniform Civil Code: A Step towards attaining Gender Justice", SSRN, April 30, 2021.

20. Id.

21. 1985 (1) SCALE 767

22. AIR 1995 SC 1531

23. Special Leave Petition (Civil) No. 2047 of 1985

24. Minattur, Joseph. "THE STORY OF A CIVIL CODE." Journal of the Indian Law Institute, vol. 18, no. 1, 1976, pp. 149-52. JSTOR.

25. Krishnayan Sen. "Uniform Civil Code." Economic and Political Weekly, vol. 39, no. 37, 2004, pp. 4196-4196. JSTOR.

CHAPTER 7

Paving a Better Future for India

We have extensively discussed the ins and outs of Uniform Civil Code. We have understood so far how the Code in its entirety is closely linked to freedom of religion and have looked at its history in detail. We have come to realised that India has a rich history of multiculturalism and diversity, and the society of India has been evolving continuously. However, before any legislation is enacted, there are several rounds of research conducted. Throughout this process, there may be several rounds of research, review, and revision, as well as public hearings and consultations with stakeholders, to ensure that the legislation is effective, fair, and in line with existing laws and policies [1]. In short, the piece of legislation is looked into to understand the need and efficacy of the same.

On similar lines, it is pertinent that we look towards Uniform Civil Code to understand the need for the legislation. The need for such a code for the nation should be considered as we discuss this contentious issue. Understanding the benefits of uniformity is important because, let's face it, adoption of such a code won't come easily and, when it does, will require some sections of the community to give up some of their rights. Since we are from a nation where religion plays a significant role in everyone's psyche, they would have to take on the loss of a portion of their faith, which is a significant sacrifice. The necessity and effectiveness in this situation must be reasonable and significant.

In this chapter, thereby, we will be looking at the apparent benefits of the Uniform Civil Code, analyse each to understand how each one is an advantage which would make the entire process of fighting for the Uniform Civil Code so much more worth it.

First Advantage: Gender Equality

It is not unknown to anyone that gender equality is one such issue which has remained a critical one in India with women having historically faced discrimination and inequality in various aspects of their lives. Despite constitutional guarantees of equality and legal protection, women in India continue to experience gender-based violence, unequal access to education and healthcare, limited economic opportunities, and cultural biases that reinforce gender roles and stereotypes.[2]

However, we cannot come to accept such inequality as a norm in our lives and have to keep on fighting for it. Thereby, raises a need to challenge such barriers which have become "systemic" and to promote equality amongst genders in India. This requires addressing issues such as gender-based violence, including domestic violence, sexual assault, and harassment. It also involves increasing access to education and healthcare for women, ensuring equal pay and job opportunities, and promoting women's representation and leadership in various fields, including politics, business, and academia.

Efforts to promote gender equality in India must also address cultural biases that perpetuate gender roles and stereotypes, such as the preference for male children and the expectation that women will prioritize their domestic roles over their careers. Education and awareness-raising campaigns can play a crucial role in challenging these attitudes and promoting a more gender-equitable society.[3]

It is unquestionable that, achieving gender equality in India is crucial for the country's social and economic development, as well as for promoting human rights and dignity for all its citizens. In recent years, there have been several initiatives and campaigns to promote gender equality in India. For instance, the government has launched various schemes and programs to increase women's participation in the workforce, such as the Beti Bachao, Beti Padhao scheme, which aims to improve the welfare of girls and promote their education. The government has also implemented several measures to improve women's safety, such as setting up fast-track courts to handle cases of sexual violence.

Civil society organizations, activists, and celebrities have also played a significant role in promoting gender equality in India. Several campaigns, such as #MeToo and #TimesUp, have helped to raise awareness about gender-based violence and harassment and have pushed for greater accountability for perpetrators.

Despite these efforts, however, there is still a long way to go to achieve gender equality in India. For example, women's representation in politics and public life remains low, and gender-based violence continues to be a pervasive problem. Additionally, there is a need to address the intersectional nature of discrimination, such as the challenges faced by Dalit women or women from marginalized communities.

We must remember that while the government has been trying to solve this issue of gender inequality, promoting gender equality is a job which requires a multi-faceted approach, including legal and policy reforms, education and awareness-raising, and cultural transformation. By prioritizing gender equality, India can build a more just and equitable society that benefits all its citizens.

Now, the reader must be wondering why we are discussing all this in length. It is pertinent for us to understand that while the government might be making all efforts to progress towards a future where gender inequality is a thing of the past, introducing Uniform Civil Code holds instrumental value in accelerating this fight.

It is on such lines, one of the most significant advantages of Uniform Civil Code is gender equality. Personal laws in India discriminate against women in many ways. For example, under Muslim personal law, a man can have up to four wives, whereas a woman can have only one husband. The Muslim Personal Law also denies women an equal share of inheritance. The Uniform Civil Code would ensure that all citizens, irrespective of their gender and religion, have equal rights and opportunities. The Uniform Civil Code would promote gender equality and ensure that women are not discriminated against in any way.[4]

By repealing discriminatory legislation, the Uniform Civil Code may alleviate gender disparity in a number of important ways. Currently, women are discriminated against in relation to marriage, divorce, and inheritance due to various personal rules for various religions. The discriminatory clauses might be removed by the Uniform Civil Code, which would also guarantee women's equal rights in all other areas of civil law.

By guaranteeing that women have equal access to opportunities and resources and by outlawing gender-based discrimination, the Uniform Civil Code might likewise advance gender justice. Provisions that encourage women's involvement in these and other fields where they are currently underrepresented might be among them. The Uniform Civil Code might also address discriminatory practises like dowry, which are still common in some regions of India.

By defending women's rights, the Uniform Civil Code might also aid in addressing gender inequity. The Uniform Civil Code could have clauses that safeguard women's rights, such as the right to education, the principle of equal pay for equal labour, and protection from domestic abuse. These rules would guarantee that women had equal access to opportunities and resources as well as protection against gender-based discrimination. [5]

Thereby, we can see that achieving gender equality could be a major advantage of Uniform Civil Code. We cannot forget that the road to gender equality in India is one which is long and hard, we might stumble on it a couple of times but Uniform Civil Code could prove to be a significantly important friend which could help us achieve what our nation has been working towards for ages now.

Second Advantage: National Integration

National integration is an ongoing challenge in India due to its diversity in terms of religion, language, culture, and ethnicity. India is home to multiple religions and ethnic groups, and there are often tensions and conflicts between these groups. In addition, there are economic disparities between different regions and communities, which can further exacerbate these tensions.

One of the key issues facing India's national integration is the persistence of communalism and sectarianism. Communalism refers to the tendency of individuals and groups to identify primarily with their religious community rather than with the nation as a whole. This can lead to conflicts between different religious groups and create divisions within society. Another challenge to national integration in India is the persistence of regionalism. Different regions in India have their own distinct cultures, languages, and identities, and there is often a tension between these regional identities and a broader national identity. This can lead to conflicts over issues such as the distribution of resources, representation in government, and cultural expression.

To address these challenges, India has adopted various policies and measures aimed at promoting national integration. These include measures to promote cultural and linguistic diversity, affirmative action policies to promote the inclusion of disadvantaged groups, and efforts to foster a sense of national identity and unity. One of the key strategies for promoting national integration in India has been the adoption of a federal system of governance, which allows for a certain degree of autonomy for different regions while maintaining a strong central government. The Constitution of India also guarantees certain fundamental rights to all citizens, regardless of their religion or ethnicity, which helps to promote a sense of national unity.

The promotion of secularism is another important strategy for promoting national integration in India. The Constitution of India recognizes the right to freedom of religion and prohibits discrimination on the basis of religion, thereby promoting a secular and inclusive society. However, there have been concerns about the rise of religious extremism and communalism in recent years, which pose a threat to national integration. [6]

Another important aspect of national integration in India is the promotion of economic development and social welfare. India has made significant progress in reducing poverty and improving access to basic services such as healthcare and education, which can help to promote a sense of inclusion and belonging among different communities. However, there is still a long way to go in addressing the economic disparities between different regions and communities in India.

Due to India's famous "diversity" and the continuation of communalism and regionalism, national integration in that country is a complicated and continuous task. However, India may continue to work towards establishing a more inclusive and harmonious society by combining policies and practises that support cultural diversity, secularism, economic growth, and social welfare. To overcome the difficulties of national integration in India and build a more inclusive and harmonious society, however, much more work has to be done.

One of the most practical answers has emerged: the adoption of the Uniform Civil Code.

The concept of Uniform Civil Code is rooted in the idea of a "common national identity". Whilst speaking in favour of implementation of Uniform Civil Code in India, learned K.M. Munshi in the Constituent Assembly remarked:

"[T]here are many factors - and important factors - which still offer serious dangers to our <u>national consolidation</u>, and it is very necessary that the whole of our life, so far as it is restricted to secular spheres, must be unified in such a way that as early as possible, we may be able to say, Well, we are not merely a nation because we say so, but also in effect, by the way we live, by our personal law, we are a strong and consolidated nation." [7]

This is imperative when we speak of integration of the nation. If we examine the issue of Uniform Civil Code through this lens, it may have some potential in creating a unified Indian identity. However, it is equally important to take into account its impact on other identities, such as regional and religious identities, which are often significant to individuals and communities. Additionally, as Bhikhu Parekh has noted, "*Identity is a result of the conscious and unconscious interaction between the range of choices provided by the larger society and our understanding of ourselves*". [8]

Therefore, it is important to consider the interplay between inter-group equality and the religious identity of minority communities when discussing the Uniform Civil Code in India and it being a solution for national integration.

It has been widely discussed that India is a diverse country, with different religions and cultures coexisting. However, the existence of different personal laws creates disparities and leads to communal tension. The Uniform Civil Code would help in promoting national integration by treating all citizens equally, irrespective of their religion, caste, and gender. The uniformity in laws would ensure that justice is served to all citizens fairly and impartially.

The Uniform Civil Code is seen by some as a means of promoting national unity in India by creating a shared legal framework that would help to reduce divisions along religious and communal lines. Currently, India follows a system of personal laws that varies based on an individual's religion, leading to different laws and practices for different communities. The Uniform Civil Code would establish a uniform standard for civil matters such as marriage, divorce, inheritance, and adoption that would apply equally to all citizens regardless of their religion.

By creating a common civil code for all citizens of India, the Uniform Civil Code would promote a shared sense of citizenship and identity, which is essential for national unity. The Uniform Civil Code would create a level playing field for all citizens, irrespective of their religious beliefs, and would help to foster a sense of belonging to a larger national community.

Third Advantage: Intergroup Religious Equality

The Indian population is comprised of a majority of Hindus and minority groups including Muslims, Christians, Sikhs, Buddhists, and Jains. In order to protect the interests of religious minorities, the Indian Constitution explicitly prohibits discrimination based on religion among citizens. [9] Furthermore, the Constitution declares India as a secular state and provides minority groups with the freedom to manage their religious affairs and cultural rights. These measures are intended to assure minority groups that they will be treated equally with the majority and that their unique religious identity will be safeguarded from assimilation into a national identity. However, when viewed through the lens of liberal multicultural theory, it becomes clear that these protections not only fail to provide substantive equality for minority groups but also present a constant threat to their religious identity. [10]

By ensuring equal treatment under the law, the introduction of a Uniform Civil Code might encourage intergroup religious equality. Different personal laws for many religions currently lead to uneven legal treatment, especially for women and minority groups. All citizens would get equal treatment under the law under a Uniform Civil Code, regardless of their gender, caste, or religion. By giving all people an equal chance to succeed, this would support intergroup religious equality.

With elimination of exclusionary clauses from personal laws, the introduction of a Uniform Civil Code might advance intergroup religious equality. Discriminatory clauses in various personal laws for various religions violate the concepts of equality and fairness. For instance, the Hindu Succession Act and the Muslim Personal Law contain various laws that discriminate against women when it comes to inheritance. These discriminatory clauses would be removed by a Uniform Civil Code, which would also guarantee that all people are treated equally. Making sure that no citizen is treated unfairly according to their caste or religion will encourage intergroup religious equality.

Through supporting gender equality, a Uniform Civil Code may advance intergroup religious equality. Discriminatory measures in various personal laws for various religions lead to gender inequity. These discriminatory clauses would be removed by a Uniform Civil Code, which would also guarantee equal rights and opportunities for women. By guaranteeing that women from all religions and castes have the same rights and opportunities, this would encourage intergroup religious equality. [11]

The adoption of a Uniform Civil Code might advance societal cohesion and intergroup religious equality. Currently, conflicts and divides between many religious communities are brought on by various personal laws for various religions. A Uniform Civil Code would foster social peace by establishing a system of civil laws that would apply to all citizens. By fostering a sense of cohesion and belonging among all Indian people, this would assist in easing tensions between various religious communities and promote intergroup religious equality.

By encouraging religious tolerance, a Uniform Civil Code might advance intergroup religious equality. Different personal rules for several religions might currently foster a feeling of superiority among followers of one religion over followers of another. By ensuring that all citizens, regardless of religion or caste, are subject to the same civil rules, a Uniform Civil Code would encourage religious tolerance. By encouraging tolerance and equality for all castes and religions, this would advance intergroup religious equality. [12]

The adoption of a uniform civil code might advance intergroup religious equality in India, to sum up. Equal treatment under the law, the elimination of discriminatory clauses from personal laws, the advancement of gender equality, social peace, religious tolerance, economic expansion and advancement, advancement of knowledge and innovation, secularism, and protection of human rights would all be promoted. Implementation is a complicated matter that necessitates protracted discussion and engagement among many religious communities and stakeholders. A Uniform Civil Code, however, maybe a huge step in advancing intergroup religious equality in India with the proper strategy and implementation.

Fourth Advantage: Improve India's global image

We have extensively talked about how India is a country with a population which is quite diverse, comprises of people coming from varied backgrounds, ethnicities, cultures and religions. India has a diversified population made up of individuals from many cultures, faiths, and ethnic groups. [13] However, because of this variety, there are also inequalities in civil laws due to various personal laws based on religion. The adoption of a Uniform Civil Code could be the answer to this problem.

There are several reasons why a unified civil code might enhance India's reputation globally. First off, it would demonstrate to the rest of the world that India is a nation which is progressive and modern, committed to its promise of secularism. Second, it would promote tourism and international investment. Thirdly, it would contribute to recovering the image of India which has been tarnished by incidents of communal violence and religious intolerance and emerge as one which is tolerant and welcoming gender equality.

India is a secular nation, and the adoption of a Uniform Civil Code will reinforce that commitment. It would convey to the rest of the world that India appreciates diversity but does not accept caste or religious prejudice. India's reputation as a contemporary, progressive society that supports justice and equality for all of its residents might benefit from this. One of the guiding principles of India's democracy is secularism. This idea will be strengthened, and

India's society would become more inclusive and democratic with the adoption of a standard civil code.

A Uniform Civil Code will demonstrate to the outside world that India is a contemporary, forward-thinking nation. India would become a more alluring place for international investment and tourists as a result. By fostering economic expansion and progress, the Uniform Civil Code may also contribute to a better perception of India abroad. Currently, it is challenging for companies to function in India due to various personal rules for various religions. This is because businesses must traverse various rules for various areas, which may be expensive and time-consuming. The adoption of a Uniform Civil Code will make the legal environment for companies more straightforward and easier for them to operate in India. This will enhance India's reputation as a nation that welcomes industry and is dedicated to economic prosperity.

Religious intolerance and acts of communal violence have damaged India's reputation abroad. By establishing a single set of civil rules that would apply to all people, a Uniform Civil Code might help ease conflicts between various faith communities. No matter their caste or religion, all Indian residents would have a greater feeling of belonging as a result. Additionally, this will enhance India's standing as a nation dedicated to harmony, peace, and tolerance across the world. Further, as discussed earlier in this chapter, Uniform Civil Code could pave the way for gender equality in India which further improve India's global image.

Fifth Advantage: Simplification of Laws

It is challenging for people to comprehend the law and obtain justice in India since the legal system is complicated and has many overlapping rules. Additionally, the judicial system's complexity raises litigation costs and causes delays in the administration of justice. This justifies the necessity for legislation simplification.

The legal system may become more effective and open to all parties by simplifying the laws. Additionally, it can make the justice system more transparent and less corrupt. By consolidating, codifying, and updating the current laws, getting rid of unnecessary, and making sure that the laws are expressed in plain and understandable language, laws may be made simpler.

Additionally, a more straightforward legal structure can boost foreign investment and improve the economic climate in India. Therefore, for India to flourish economically, rules must be made simpler. Additionally, it can be challenging for the general public, particularly those with less education or who belong to marginalised populations, to comprehend and navigate the legal system due to the lengthy and complicated legal processes. This exacerbates the issue of cases pending in court by leading to either delayed justice or no justice at all. [14]

Moreover, India has a federal system of governance, which means that both the central and state governments can make laws on different subjects. This leads to a multitude of laws on the same subject, resulting in confusion and inconsistencies in the legal system. Further, some of these laws are outdated and no longer relevant, but remain in the books, adding to the complexity of the legal system.

We thus understand that simplification of laws is the need of the hour in India. Uniform Civil Code is one of the mediums through which India can work towards simplification of laws. India currently has a complicated and perplexing legal system. The personal laws of many faiths result in a diversity of rules governing marriage, divorce, inheritance, and other civic concerns. As a result, people could be subject to various laws depending on their faith, which causes confusion and conflict. By establishing a single set of civil rules that all people, regardless of their faith, would be bound by, a Uniform Civil Code would streamline the judicial system.

The adoption of the Uniform Civil Code would advance legal consistency in India. Laws that are uniform would encourage uniformity in court rulings and decrease legal conflicts. Additionally, it would make legal procedures simpler and ease the judiciary's workload. By doing this, the judicial system would become more effective and open to the public. Further, it would promote accountability, reduce corruption, and create a more favourable environment for business and investment- as we would discuss consequently.

Sixth Advantage: Reduction in Corruption

In India, corruption is a serious issue that hurts many facets of society, including the judicial system. In India, a complex legal system with distinct rules for several religions has resulted from the existence of personal laws based on various religions. As a result, there is a fertile environment for corruption since people may take advantage of legal quirks and anomalies to further their interests. To streamline India's legal system and lower corruption, the adoption of a Uniform Civil Code is a potential solution.

In India, a complex legal system with distinct rules for several religions has resulted from the existence of personal laws based on various religions. Complex laws and regulations can create opportunities for corruption by allowing officials to interpret laws in their way or demand bribes for providing services. By establishing a single set of civil rules that all people, regardless of their faith, would be bound by, a Uniform Civil Code would streamline the judicial system. [15]

The likelihood of extortion and bribery would decrease with the introduction of a Uniform Civil Code. Legal conflicts and delays are currently a result of India's complicated and challenging legal system. By demanding extortionate payments or proposing bribes, people might take advantage of legal ambiguities and inconsistencies to hasten the judicial process. These dishonest practices would be less likely to occur under a more straightforward legal structure.

Seventh Advantage: Catalyst for Business and Investment

India has emerged as one of the fastest-growing economies in the world. The country's business and investment climate, however, continues to be difficult due to several problems, including a complicated legal system, a lack of transparency, and inconsistent legislation among states. A Uniform Civil Code has been advocated as a means of streamlining the legal system, lowering legal conflicts, and fostering uniformity in state legislation.

Different laws are in place for each religion in India's existing complicated and fragmented legal system. As a result, people may be subject to varying regulatory requirements and prohibitions depending on their faith, which creates a complex business and investment climate. Complex and unclear laws can discourage investment and business development by creating uncertainty and increasing transaction costs. The adoption of a Uniform Civil Code would streamline the legal system by creating a single set of civil laws that would apply to all citizens, regardless of their faith. For investors and companies, this would level the playing field and encourage consistency and openness. [16]

We must understand that India's present legal system is time and money-consuming. Legal snags and disagreements sometimes lead to hefty legal fees, which deters firms and investors from making investments in the nation. A less complicated legal system would result in fewer legal conflicts, saving time and money while improving the effectiveness and accessibility of the legal system for companies and investors. This would stimulate economic growth and boost investment.

At the core, Uniform Civil Code, by reducing the complexity of laws in India allow investors to comfortably enter the market and explore for the ample amount of business opportunities housed by our country. It allows for a more transparent system which would make it simpler for firms and investors to comprehend their legal rights and duties. A Uniform Civil Code would offer stability and clarity in civil affairs, simplifying business and investment operations in the nation. This will increase legal clarity and lessen legal conflicts, improving the business and investment climate in India. Further, as discussed above, Uniform Civil Code makes way for the enhancement of the image of India at a global level, which is bound to open our country to opportunities and investment.

Eighth Advantage: Make law accessible and comprehensible.

The implementation of the Uniform Civil Code can help in simplifying laws in India by replacing the existing personal laws of various religions with a common set of laws applicable to all citizens irrespective of their religion. This would eliminate the complexity and confusion arising out of the existence of multiple personal laws that differ from one another, creating disparities in the rights and obligations of individuals based on their religion.

By implementing a uniform civil code, there would be a single set of laws governing aspects such as marriage, divorce, inheritance, and adoption for all citizens, eliminating the need for separate laws based on religion. This would make the legal system more efficient, accessible, and transparent to the common man.

Currently, matters such as marriage, divorce, inheritance, and adoption are governed by personal laws that vary according to religious communities in India. This makes the legal system complicated to navigate, especially for those who may need to access legal remedies. A single legal framework for personal matters, among others would allow the common man to be able to easily navigate the legal system of India.

The implementation of a Uniform Civil Code would bring about harmonization of laws and simplify the legal system, making it more accessible and comprehensible to people. It would eliminate the need for multiple legal systems and ensure that all individuals are governed by the same laws, regardless of their religion.

Opinions on Adoption of Uniform Civil Code

Over the years, Uniform Civil Code has been advocated for by a number of people. They have opined on the issue and herein we would be looking at their opinions in particular. When we are looking at the utility of the Uniform Civil Code, it is pertinent that we look at the discussions around the same in the Constituent Assembly Debates and thereby we would be starting from thereon.

Article 35 of the Draft Constitution originally included the Uniform Civil Code. However, there was a demand to add a proviso to make the Uniform Civil Code non-obligatory and keep personal laws outside its purview. The proviso stated that any group, section, or community with their own personal law would not be required to give it up. Despite being seen as a threat to religious freedoms, there were many reasons given in support of a common civil code. K.M. Munshi strongly opposed the idea that the majority should dominate over minorities, stating that:

"It is not therefore correct to say that such an act is tyranny of the majority. If you will look at the countries in Europe which have a Civil Code, everyone who goes there from any part of the world and every minority, has to submit to the Civil Code. It is not felt to be tyrannical to the minority. The point however is this, whether we are going to consolidate and unify our personal law in

such a way that the way of life of the whole country may in course of time be unified and secular. We want to divorce religion from personal law, from what may be called social relations or from the rights of parties as regards inheritance or succession. What have these things got to do with religion I really fail to understand."
[17]

Munshi argued for the unifying force of secularism, proposing that a single way of life should be adopted by all, but this view is highly controversial as it seems to silence the voice of diversity. Another reason for supporting the Uniform Civil Code was the empowerment of women. Since the right to equality was already recognized as one of the most fundamental rights, the unequal treatment of genders under personal laws could no longer be justified. Therefore, practices that undermined women's right to equality would have to be eliminated. A common civil law governing personal matters would bring all women under one umbrella, and regardless of race or religion, discriminatory practices would be abolished.

In contrast, Shri Alladi Krishnaswamy Ayyar provides a more practical reason for aiming for a Uniform Civil Code, based on the fallacy of strictly segregated existence of different communities. He argues that in a country like India, there is a great deal of interaction between various communities, which often leads to conflicts between specific personal laws. In addition, one legal system is often influenced by another legal system. He opined that:

"In very many matters today the sponsors of the Hindu Code have taken a lead not from Hindu Law alone, but from other systems also. Similarly, the Succession Act has drawn upon both the Roman and the English systems. Therefore, no system can be self-contained, if it is to have in it the elements of growth. Our ancients did not think of a unified nation to be welded together into a democratic whole. There is no use clinging always to the past. We are departing from the past in regard to an important particular, namely, we want the whole of India to be welded and united together as a single nation. Are we helping those factors which help the welding together into a single nation, or is this country to be kept up always as a series of competing communities? That is the question at issue."

The concept of cultural relativity is challenged by Ayyar, who questions the drawbacks of having separate personal laws governed entirely by religion, which can have multiple interpretations. He argues that this approach limits the potential for reform. Ayyar extends the concept of uniformity beyond a necessary evil, in contrast to Munshi, who cited examples of other Islamic countries where the forceful application of the majoritarian law was considered justified if it brought reform.

Further, Justice V.R. Krishna Iyer has spoken in favour of Uniform Civil Code. He was a former judge of the Supreme Court of India who was known for his progressive views. He believed that the Uniform Civil Code was necessary to promote national integration and gender justice. In an interview with The Hindu, he said, "*A common civil code is necessary for gender justice and national unity*"[19].

MJ Akbar, a journalist, author, and former member of the Indian Parliament, has spoken extensively on the subject. He believes that the Uniform Civil Code is necessary to create a modern and secular India. In an article for The Times of India, he opined, "*A uniform civil code will provide India with the necessary modernity and a secular ethos. It will help the country to move forward in a globalized world*"[20].

More importantly, our Prime Minister, Mr. Narendra Modi has expressed his support for Uniform Civil Code. He believes that it to be a necessary for integration of the nation. In a speech at a rally in Uttar Pradesh, he expressed, "*We need to have a common civil code for the sake of national unity and to promote gender justice.*"[21]

Opinion of Ambedkar on Uniform Civil Code

Ambedkar was a strong advocate of Uniform Civil Code, rejecting the notion that it was impossible to implement in a vast country like India. He pointed out that the only area lacking a uniform law was that of marriage and succession, while other areas of civil law, such as transfer of property, contract, and the sale of goods, were already uniform in nature. Ambedkar was a reformist who believed in Western models of law and social relations to bring about social change in the Indian context. Unlike Munshi, he did not support adding a proviso to the unenforceable Article 35 but instead advocated for the gradual inclusion of communities with their voluntary consent once the legislature fulfills its promise to implement a Uniform Civil Code. He opined that:

"I quite realise their feelings in the matter, but I think they have read rather too much into article 35, which merely proposes that the State shall endeavour to secure a civil code for the citizens of the country. It does not say that after the Code is framed the State shall enforce it upon all citizens merely because they are citizens. It is perfectly possible that the future parliament may make a provision by way of making a beginning that the Code shall apply only to those who make a declaration that they are prepared to be bound by it, so that in the initial stage the application of the Code may be purely voluntary.

Parliament may feel the ground by some such method. This is not a novel method." [22]

Ambedkar, a staunch critic of the Hindu religion, had denounced casteism and untouchability as dogmas that infested Hinduism as early as 1936. However, in the Constituent Assembly, he refuted the notion that the Uniform Civil Code was a tool for the majority or the tyranny of the majority. He cited the example of the Shariat Act, 1936, which was applied uniformly to all Muslims in India and was welcomed by them as a convenient uniform law. The Act brought Muslims who were previously governed by Hindu laws in specific areas under a uniform law, which was beneficial for them. Similarly, if certain principles of Hinduism were incorporated into the Uniform Civil Code, it would not be because they belonged to Hinduism but because they were suitable for a progressive society. Ambedkar argued that this should not be seen as a tyranny of the majority. He stated that:

"Therefore if it was found necessary that to evolve a single civil code applicable to all citizens irrespective of their religion, certain portions of the Hindus law, not because they were contained in Hindu law but because they were found to be the most suitable, were incorporated into the new civil code projected by article 35, I am quite certain that it would not be open to any

Muslim to say that the framers of the civil code had done great violence to the sentiments of the Muslim community." [23]

Ambedkar's statement is a clear testament to his dedication to the implementation of a Uniform Civil Code that would bring about crucial changes in the personal lives of all Indians, regardless of their religion or community. His relentless effort to pass the Hindu Code Bills after independence, which ultimately led to his resignation from the cabinet, further attests to his determination to establish a Uniform Civil Code. Despite the failure to pass the proposed amendment to article 35, there was no clear majority on the Uniform Civil Code issue, and some of the concerns expressed during those debates are still relevant in the discussions on the subject today, as evidenced by the debates in 2016.

Conclusion

In this chapter we have discussed at length on why our country needs to implement the uniform civil code. One of the main reasons is to promote the principle of equality enshrined in the Constitution of India by ensuring that all citizens, regardless of their religion, are subject to the same laws in personal matters such as marriage, divorce, adoption, and inheritance. The current system of personal laws, which are based on religious customs and practices, often perpetuate gender inequality and discrimination against women.

A uniform civil code would also help in fostering national unity and integration by providing a common legal framework for all citizens of the country. It would help in promoting social harmony and reducing inter-community tensions by eliminating the perception of differential treatment of different religious communities. Moreover, the existence of different personal laws based on religious practices and customs often leads to confusion and conflict, especially in cases involving inter-faith marriages and succession. A uniform civil code would help in resolving such conflicts by providing a clear legal framework for resolution.

Uniform Civil Code is at its very core, a call to eradicate the diseases which have made their home in our society, whether it be gender related or religion related. While we work towards resolution of the issues at hand, through implementation of the Civil Code, we must seek to address two questions primarily.

The first question that arises is how to establish uniformity in personal laws without disregarding the uniqueness of each community. It is important to examine whether we perceive the practices of a particular community as backward and unjust without serious consideration. If we do not address these concerns, we may fall into the same trap as the Americans who saw the indigenous population as savages who needed to be rescued by the progressive, civilized norms of Christianity.

The second question is whether uniformity has succeeded in eliminating gender inequalities that continue to diminish the status of women in our society. This question is related to the previous one. The definition of inequality may vary from one community to another, and it is important to identify the different layers of gender injustices and inequalities that operate within each society. Personal laws of a particular community may contain elements that are contradictory to the notion of gender equality within that society. Therefore, the first step should be to eliminate these unjust practices that are unique to that community. Instead of hastily creating a uniform definition of injustice and inequality, which is the dominant point of view, it is necessary for each society to first acknowledge the definitions of inequality and injustice within their particular sphere of life. Otherwise, communities may become defensive against the demands of uniformity, and injustices within their own communities may go unnoticed.

While working for the betterment of our society, we must keep in mind that change is a slow process, and we cannot fast track everything in life. These constant calls for Uniform Civil Code are ultimately a wakeup call for us to make the requisite changes in the system of personal laws and focus on resolution of the issues.

End Notes

1. Jennifer Smookler, "Making a Difference? The Effectiveness of Pre-Legislative Scrutiny", *Parliamentary Affairs*, Volume 59, Issue 3, July 2006, Pages 522–535

2. John, Thomas. "Succession Law in India and Obstacles in the Road to Gender Equality" *Student Bar Review, vol. 18, no. 2, 2006*, pp. 38–58. JSTOR.

3. Ojha, Purnima. "WOMEN'S ISSUES IN INDIA: ROLE AND IMPORTANCE OF MEDIA." *The Indian Journal of Political Science*, vol. 72, no. 1, 2011, pp. 87–102. *JSTOR*.

4. Rattan, Jyoti. "UNIFORM CIVIL CODE IN INDIA: A BINDING OBLIGATION UNDER INTERNATIONAL AND DOMESTIC LAW." *Journal of the Indian Law Institute*, vol. 46, no. 4, 2004, pp. 577–87. *JSTOR*.

5. Menon, Nivedita. "A Uniform Civil Code in India: The State of the Debate in 2014." *Feminist Studies*, vol. 40, no. 2, 2014, pp. 480–86. *JSTOR*.

6. Singh, Akhilendra Pratap. "UTILITY OF UNIFORM CIVIL CODE." *Journal of the Indian Law Institute*, vol. 59, no. 2, 2017, pp. 178–87. *JSTOR*.

7. K.M. Munshi, Constituent Assembly debates, Volume VII, dated September 27, 1949.

8. Bhikhu Parekh,"Identity, Culture and Dialogue" (1992).

9. Aiyar, Mani Shankar. "Politics and Religion in India." India International Centre Quarterly, vol. 34, no. 1, 2007, pp. 42–50. JSTOR.

10. Neha Sehgal, "Religion in India: Tolerance and Segregation" Pew Research Centre

11. Manooja, D. C. "UNIFORM CIVIL CODE: A SUGGESTION." Journal of the Indian Law Institute, vol. 42, no. 2/4, 2000, pp. 448–57. JSTOR.

12. Id.

13. DESOUZA, PETER RONALD. "Politics of the Uniform Civil Code in India." *Economic and Political Weekly*, vol. 50, no. 48, 2015, pp. 50–57. *JSTOR*.

14. Mishra, Anumeha. "Review of UNIFORM CIVIL CODE FOR INDIA: PROPOSED BLUEPRINT FOR SCHOLARLY DISCOURSE" *Journal of the Indian Law Institute*, vol. 58, no. 3, 2016, pp. 386–90. *JSTOR*.

15. Supra note 11.

16. Choudhary, Richa, "Uniform Civil Code for India?", SSRN, July 12, 2020.

17. Supra note 7

18. Shri Alladi Krishnaswamy Ayyar, Constituent Assembly debates, Volume VII, dated December 2, 1948.

19. V. Venkatesan "A civil code is necessary for gender justice, says Justice Krishna Iyer", The Hindu, 2010

20. MJ Akbar, "UCC will provide India with necessary modernity", The Times of India, 2014

21. Press Trust of India "Need uniform civil code for national unity, gender justice: PM Modi", Business Standard, 2017

22. Dr. B. R. Ambedkar "Thoughts on Linguistic States", Ch 7, published in 1955.

23. Dr. B. R. Ambedkar, Constituent Assembly Debates, Volume VII, 1st November 1948.

CHAPTER 8

From The Lens of Indian Women

The personal laws governing social institutions like marriage and family in India have always been closely tied to the human rights of women. It is these laws which precisely dictate the legal framework for the status of women within such institutions, and as such, are critical to ensuring their rights. There is no doubt to the fact that our country is a highly diverse nation, with a complex and heterogeneous population which have their own way of dealing with such institutions. Such categories are not mutually exclusive and often overlap, creating a highly dynamic and colorful society which is challenging to manage.

Thereby we must expect that a Kashmiri Brahmin woman's experience will differ significantly from that of a Sarayupari Brahmin woman, and a Brahmin woman in West Bengal will have different social and religious norms than a

Bengali low-caste woman or a Namboodiri Brahmin in Kerala. While all these women may face patriarchal oppression from afar, a closer look reveals that what may appear similar is often quite different in form and nature. To many, in a country as diverse as India, the idea of a uniform personal law seems difficult in as a solution to address the human rights issues faced by women in relation to social institutions such as marriage and family. To them the concept of uniformity being often touted as a means of eradicating the repressive practices which are embedded in India's existing personal laws seems to be a far-fetched dream. [1]

However, it is pertinent that we remember that the Indian Constitution envisions a Uniform Civil Code as a viable solution for the social problems which India faces. The Supreme Court of India has consistently reminded the legislature of the promise of a Uniform Civil Code, which was deferred to the future by the framers of the Constitution. Yes, we must remember that in a society as diverse as India, it is important to recognize that the experiences of women from different communities can vary widely, and that the imposition of uniformity may not necessarily be the best solution to address the complexities of personal law. Yet, we must not discard the idea that the Uniform Civil Code might just be what Indian women have been on the look out for all these years.

The issue of gender justice in personal laws has been a contentious topic and has been cited as a reason to implement Uniform Civil Code, particularly after several Supreme Court decisions on the matter. The demand for Uniform Civil Code comes from both right-wing Hindu socio-political groups and women's rights groups, but their intentions for the demand differ significantly. These groups also argue for equality, claiming that if legislative interference is allowed in Hindu personal laws, it should also be allowed in Muslim personal laws. However, this argument is not convincing, given the discrepancy between social and legal realities. Werner Menski, an expert on Hindu law, explains this disconnect, stating that:

[H]indu Law has always been a reflection of the way of life of millions of very diverse people.... What was abolished by the formal law was manifestly only a fragment of the field, not the entire social reality of Hindu Law. [2]

The implementation of a Uniform Civil Code has been demanded as a means to achieve gender justice in personal laws. The former argue that the codification and amendment of Hindu personal laws have made them gender just, and that if interference is allowed in Hindu personal laws, it should also be allowed in Muslim personal laws. However, this argument is flawed, as the legislative interference in Hindu personal laws has not significantly improved the position of women in Hindu society. Similarly, the implementation of reformed Muslim personal laws is not guaranteed to be accepted and practiced by the Muslim community.

This political interpretation of gender justice by Hindu socio-political groups discredits the legitimate demands of women's rights groups for equal rights in personal laws. While the Indian Constitution grants religious groups the freedom to manage their own affairs, this cannot be used as an excuse to deny equal rights to women. Religious groups must recognize that their conservative social norms have discriminated against women, and that they cannot deny equal status to a group that is part of their own larger group. Therefore, viewed from the perspective of intra-group equality and gender justice, the demand for Uniform Civil Code seems to be justified. [3]

However, not all agree with such view. Flavia Agnes offers a satisfactory solution regarding the usefulness of the Uniform Civil Code in promoting gender justice in personal laws, taking into account the situation of Hindu women following the codification of Hindu personal laws.

"[T]he lessons learnt in the last 60 years are that uniformity has not worked. It has also had a disastrous

impact on the rights of Hindu women... Rather than excluding women from the realm of rights, we need to adopt an inclusive approach... so that women at the margins are not deprived of their right to a life with dignity and sustenance by adopting moralistic principles that are alien to cultural ethos and customary practices..... Rather than uniformity, what women need are an accessible and affordable justice delivery system and inclusive models of development that will help to eliminate their poverty and destitution and help to build an egalitarian world." [4]

Agnes's observation reveals that uniformity has not significantly improved the position of women in Hindu society. Therefore, it would be reasonable to assume that the same may be true for women as a group in the country. The author herein, however, disagrees. As mentioned earlier, it is pertinent to note that this is just one of the viewpoints on Uniform Civil Code. It is important to note that the opinions of women in India on Uniform Civil Code are not monolithic, and some various viewpoints and concerns need to be considered while discussing the implementation of Uniform Civil Code.

While analysing the need for a uniform civil code and their impact on women, we must analyse the institutions and the impact uniformity might bring in at the various stages of life of a woman.

Thereby we would be looking at this chapter from such a perspective.

Marriage

Marriage is an institution which is deemed sacred in India. In line with personal laws and religion, there are vast differences in the way they are governed. For Hindus, Buddhists, Sikhs, and Jains in India, the Hindu Marriage Act of 1955 is applicable. This law has a number of significant clauses. First, it establishes the minimum age requirements for marriage: brides must be at least 18 years old, and grooms must be at least 21. Additionally, the law preserves the monogamy rule, which states that people can only be married to one person at a time. It also details the rites and ceremonies that must be carried out for a Hindu marriage to be regarded as legitimate. In order to prevent weddings between close blood relatives or those with close affinities, the statute further specifies banned degrees of kinship. [5]

Muslims in India abide under sharia, the personal laws of Islam. Muslim personal law applies to a few important features of Muslim marriages. One essential element is that for a marriage to be regarded legal, both the bride and the groom must consent. Muslim personal law also permits polygamy, enabling Muslim males to have up to four wives, if certain requirements are met. In addition, the groom must provide the bride with a monetary gift or payment known as the Mehr as a sort of security. The nikah, or solemnization, of a Muslim marriage usually happens in front of witnesses. [6]

The Parsi Marriage and Divorce Act of 1936 regulates Parsi weddings, whereas the Indian Christian Marriage Act of 1872 governs Christian unions. Different features of marriage in different civilizations are outlined by these laws. The concept of monogamy is upheld by both Christian and Parsi law, ensuring that people are only allowed to have one marriage at a time. These regulations also mandate that weddings be solemnised using certain religious rites accepted by the groups involved. Additionally, marriage registration is required under both Christian and Parsi law for the reasons of legal recognition and recording. [7]

Different marriage laws in India can present women with a variety of obstacles and challenges, which can result in inequality and discrimination. These laws support gender inequality by giving men preferred rights and advantages while restricting the freedom and authority of decision-making for women. For instance, certain personal laws that allowed polygamy and unilateral divorce by males might expose women to exploitation and prejudice. Such disparities prevent women from properly exercising their rights and leading dignified lives.

The restricted rights and protections granted to women by various marriage laws is another important problem. In areas including marriage, divorce, maintenance, custody, and inheritance, women may experience inequities. Religion based personal laws sometimes fall short of offering equal protection for women's rights, leaving them without suitable legal options in circumstances of abuse, marital strife, or property issues. This may make it harder for women to get the justice and protection they need and prolong a cycle of vulnerability.

Different marriage rules may also cause societal shame and marginalisation for women. Women may experience social pressure and prejudice based on their religious background in situations where personal laws give unequal rights or practises. This may lead to a lack of access to social support networks, educational chances, and career prospects. Such societal stigmatisation further impairs women's ability to advance both personally and professionally. [8]

The difficulties experienced by women are exacerbated by the intricacy of navigating various legal processes across various marital laws. It becomes difficult for women to grasp their rights and navigate through multiple legal systems, especially if they need to file legal claims under numerous personal laws. This intricacy frequently serves as a barrier, restricting women's access to justice and preventing them from standing up for their rights.

It is crucial to work towards a fairer and more consistent legal framework that promotes women's rights and supports gender equality in order to solve these issues. The adoption of a Uniform Civil Code is a viable remedy to lessen the challenges brought on by various marriage laws and support a more equitable and inclusive society.

The Code would promote equality and non-discrimination by doing rid of the differences in marriage laws based on religion, guaranteeing that women have the same rights and protections regardless of their religious background. As a result, gender gaps would be reduced, and society would become more just and egalitarian. It would do away with the difficulties that come with navigating various personal laws and offer a unified legal system that is simpler to comprehend and accessible to all citizens. By lowering the obstacles women encounter in seeking restitution, this will guarantee that they have better access to justice and legal remedies. However, any legislative change must be addressed delicately, considering the many religious and cultural practises in India, while making sure that women's rights are protected, and their empowerment is promoted.

Divorce

Divorce is another point in a woman's life which is important to her and whereby she would be looking towards law to help her instead of making it complicated by making all the provisions differ on the basis of religion.

There are two primary provisions for divorce in Hindu Personal Law, which is controlled by the Hindu Marriage Act of 1955. If both parties consent, a mutual consent divorce enables partners to dissolve their union. They must mutually agree on the conditions of divorce and live apart for a certain amount of time. There is also the option for a fault-based divorce, which can be requested for reasons including cruelty, infidelity, desertion, conversion, mental insanity, or infectious illness. A divorce petitioner must present evidence in court to support their claims.

The Dissolution of Muslim Marriages Act, 1939, and conventional Islamic law are the main sources of divorce regulation in Muslim personal law. By saying "talaq" three times, the husband can unilaterally dissolve the marriage. But in 2017, the quick triple talaq practise was deemed invalid. Khula is a type of divorce when the woman initiates the process by asking for a financial settlement or giving the dowry back to the husband. For khula, the husband's approval is not necessary. [9]

The Indian Divorce Act of 1869 is followed by Christian Personal Law. For example, infidelity, cruelty, desertion, or conversion to a different faith are all valid reasons for divorce. If one spouse has engaged in adultery, a divorce may be granted; but, if the petitioner has been subjected to physical or emotional abuse, a divorce may not be granted. If one spouse has unjustifiably forsaken the other for at least two years, desertion permits divorce. If one spouse has changed to a new faith and stopped being a Christian, divorce is now possible.

The Parsi Marriage and Divorce Act, 1936 is the main statute governing Parsi Personal Law. Acts like that of infidelity, conversion, cruelty, abandonment, or terminal illness are all valid reasons for divorce. If one spouse has engaged in adultery, divorce is permissible; if the other spouse has converted to a different faith, divorce is permissible. Desertion provides for divorce if one spouse has abandoned the other for a continuous period of at least two years, while cruelty allows for divorce if one spouse has treated the other cruelly. If one spouse has been incurably insane for at least two years, it is possible to get a divorce on the grounds of incurable insanity. [10]

Similar to the problems faced due to disparities in marriage, these differences in divorce also cause problems to women. They are left juggling around the different complex provisions while being stuck in an undesirable situation. The Uniform Civil Code could act as a lifeline to women in such a situation. The Code would provide a uniform set of divorce rules that would apply to all people, regardless of their religious affiliations. By guaranteeing that men and women are subject to the same legal requirements and have similar rights and safeguards in divorce procedures, this would promote equality and non-discrimination. The current personal laws' discrepancies and inequities, wherein divorce rights and processes differ based on religious connections, will be eliminated.

Further, the Code would address the problem of gender disparity in divorce by supporting the equality of men and women in terms of rights and opportunities. It would do away with discriminatory practises that are common in several personal laws, including men's exclusive right to divorce or women's constrained possibilities. A Uniform Civil Code would support a more just and equitable society by allowing equal access to divorce and related issues including alimony, child custody, and property distribution.

Adoption

Adoption is another important step in a woman's life wherein, again, personal laws differ by a lot. The Hindu Adoption and Maintenance Act of 1956 regulates adoption under Hindu Personal Law. Adoption is permissible for any Hindu who is of sound mind and is of legal age. There are limitations for married couples adopting, though, if they already have a live child of the same gender or if one of the partners has been adopted. Hindus are able to adopt either through a formal ceremony that includes all essential rites or through a registered adoption, in which all necessary legal steps are taken, including registering the adoption with the appropriate authorities. The adopted kid has the same rights, benefits, and duties as a biological child in the adoptive family after the adoption is recognised legally, including inheritance rights. [11]

Adoption is not a subject of codified law under Muslim personal law. Instead, the Kafala concept — which denotes a type of guardianship — is used. A kid may be given to another person or family for care and custody under Kafala, but they are not legally separated from their biological family and do not gain the status of a biological child.

The Juvenile Justice (Care and Protection of Children) Act, 2015, which is applicable to all communities, including Christians, largely governs Christian adoption. This Act establishes a thorough legal framework for adoption, governing the procedure, requirements for eligibility, and duties of adoptive parents. Christian adoptive parents or couples must follow the rules set forth in this Act.

The Parsi Adoption and Maintenance Act of 1954 governs Parsi adoption. Adoption is open to Parsis of sound mind who have not already adopted a child. At least 21 years must pass between the kid and the adopted parent(s). In the Parsi culture, adoption is done through a documented procedure that entails getting the biological parents' or legal guardians' agreement, going through the required legal hoops, and registering the adoption. The adopted kid has the same rights, benefits, and duties as a biological child in the adoptive family after the adoption is recognised legally, including inheritance rights.

For women who want to adopt, the disparity in adoption rules among various personal laws can lead to misunderstanding and a lack of clarity. It can be difficult and time-consuming to navigate the complexity and variances in rules, eligibility requirements, and legal requirements. Women may find it challenging to comprehend and carry out the essential legal responsibilities due to the lack of uniformity, which can result in errors and irregularities in the adoption process. [12]

Further, adoption may be subject to special cultural and religious factors under various personal laws, which might influence women's choices and decisions. When considering adoption, women may need to negotiate extra commitments, demands, or preferences as a result of these factors. Such cultural and religious issues may constrain women's options and limit their autonomy when it comes to adoption-related decisions.

It is crucial to understand that people of all sexes and backgrounds can experience similar difficulties; they are not just experienced by women. The best interests of the child must be prioritised while guaranteeing equal chances and rights for potential adoptive parents, especially women, via the development of more inclusive and simplified adoption regulations. [13] Uniform Civil Code can prove to be a viable solution in such a scenario. By offering a standard set of rules and regulations that are applicable to all people, regardless of their gender or religion affiliation, the Code would promote equality and non-discrimination. By removing any prejudices or discriminatory practises existent in various personal laws, it would guarantee that women had equal rights and chances during the adoption process. [14]

Most importantly, in adoption procedures, a Uniform Civil Code would prioritise the child's best interests. It would set standardised standards for evaluating potential adoptive parents' eligibility, ensuring that the child's well-being, safety, and welfare are prioritised. This would establish a solid legal framework for safeguarding children's rights and ensuring their placement in supportive and caring homes.

Succession

When it comes to succession, laws vary significantly in line with religious practices. The Hindu Succession Act of 1956, as revised in 2005, significantly altered women's succession rights in Hindu families. [15] Daughters now have same rights in the ancestral property as males. In the coparcenary property, this means that daughters now have the same rights and duties as sons. In the absence of a standard civil code, the Indian Succession Act of 1925 governs succession for Christians. In terms of inheritance rights, the Act makes no distinction between males and women. Male and female heirs have equal rights to inherit a deceased person's property. As a result, women have equal succession rights in Christian personal law.

Muslim Personal Law succession rules are based on Islamic principles established from the Quran and Hadith. Daughters receive half the portion of boys in Muslim inheritance. It is crucial to note, however, that the implementation of these commandments varies between various sects and schools of thought within the Muslim community. Daughters may be entitled to a smaller share than males in specific instances. This disparity has been the topic of controversy and discussion, with requests for reform to give women with equal inheritance rights. [16]

The Parsi Succession Act of 1865 governs Parsis in India, granting men and women equal inheritance rights. In terms of property inheritance, women have the same rights as males. The Parsi community has a long tradition of offering women equal rights in succession affairs, indicating a progressive commitment to gender equality.

Such disparities in succession for women puts them in a difficult situation. Women may experience economic disadvantages in personal laws where women get a less portion of inheritance than males, such as in Muslim personal law. This can limit their access to property, assets, and financial resources, all of which are critical for their economic empowerment and independence. Unequal inheritance can perpetuate gender gaps and support patriarchal norms, making it more difficult for women to gain financial security and control over their life. [17]

Women who have restricted or no inheritance rights may become financially dependent on male relatives or heirs. Women may be more prone to economic exploitation, abuse, and control as a result of their reliance. Inheritance rights deprivation might limit their alternatives and liberty, potentially placing individuals in situations where they are financially dependent on others for their wellbeing.

While Uniform Civil Code cannot change the thinking of people in India, it can definitely help women stand at an equal footing when it comes to succession. The Code holds immense power in bring about gender equality in the most absolute and important sense- allowing women to enjoy economic independence and empowering them to make important financial decisions. It would reduce uncertainty and conflicts by providing a clear explanation of inherited rights, processes, and legal duties. This would make it simpler for women to express their rights and traverse the legal system, resulting in fewer legal challenges and a more efficient and transparent procedure. [18]

Equal inheritance rights under a Uniform Civil Code would aid women's economic independence. Inheritance may give women access to property, assets, and financial resources, allowing them to start enterprises, invest, and plan for their future. Their autonomy, decision-making capacity, and overall well-being would benefit from economic empowerment. By questioning established gender roles and conventions that perpetuate injustice, a Uniform Civil Code would promote social equality and empowerment. Equal inheritance rights would call into question cultural beliefs that undervalue women's efforts and maintain their disadvantaged status. It would enable women to fully engage in family and communal decision-making processes, therefore raising their social standing and empowering them.

Feminist Movements and the Uniform Civil Code

In the pre-independence era, there were some demands for a Uniform Civil Code from the women's movement. However, it was in the 1970s when the issue gained momentum and the women's movement started supporting the introduction of a Uniform Civil Code to achieve gender justice. At that time, the feminist pro- Uniform Civil Code position was not seen as distinct from the mainstream discourse of national integration, but rather considered part of the same project. The Committee on the Status of Women in India also called for the expeditious implementation of a Uniform Civil Code, highlighting the gender inequality in personal laws and arguing that it is against the spirit of national integration. The absence of a Uniform Civil Code was seen as an incongruity that could not be justified in a secular, modern, and scientific society. [19]

However, in the 1980s, the call for the Uniform Civil Code became more differentiated among women's rights activists. While it remained a dominant position among many activists and groups, some began to rethink their argumentation. They realized that the national integrity argument was a farce as it primarily aimed to protect Hindu integrity. Women's rights activists now aimed to distinguish their envisioned Uniform Civil Code from the one proposed by the Bharatiya Janata Party. [20]

Some women's groups, such as Manushi and Saheli, called for a Uniform Civil Code based on the principles of fairness and equality, rather than as a means of promoting Hindu law. The Young Christian Women's Association (YCWA) also passed resolutions in favor of a Uniform Civil Code. [21]

Women's groups worked on drafting possible contents for a Uniform Civil Code and introducing them into parliament. One such draft envisioned a gender-just Uniform Civil Code built on three pillars: the best pro-women elements from the existing personal law systems, desirable features from the civil laws of other countries, and provisions of international conventions and agreements. Overall, there was a strong demand among feminists and women's rights groups for the implementation of a Uniform Civil Code until the mid-1980s, with hopes that parliament would take the project further.

However, slowly a shift was noticed wherein the women's movement sought to distance themselves from the entire picture. What led to the shift within the women's movement was the recognition that the secularization of laws may not be a panacea for all women's issues. The case of Shah Bano, who faced immense pressure from her community and ultimately gave up her court-approved maintenance rights, highlighted the conflict between multiple interests, obligations, and identities of religious women. [22] Kimberle Crenshaw's concept of intersectionality describes how belonging to multiple subordinate groups can result in multiple burdens and marginalization. [23] Additionally, minority women often feel compelled to choose between the conflicting political agendas pursued by the various groups to which they belong. Flavia Agnes applies this predicament to the Muslim women in India, who must choose between their claims for gender equality and their religious beliefs and community affiliations.

Although a shift away from advocating for a Uniform Civil Code is evident, there is currently no consensus on what alternative approach to take. In the 1990s, the women's movement faced a crisis regarding personal laws, with different sub-groups often conflicting with each other due to the lack of a common standpoint. [24] While the movement generally agreed that personal laws were discriminatory towards women, proposed solutions varied. Presently, many activists view the replacement of personal laws with a Uniform Civil Code, even if it is called an Egalitarian Civil Code, as a top-down approach that would harm the interests of religious women and be ineffective in improving the situation on the ground.

Conclusion

It is critical to evaluate the underlying legal concepts behind India's development of a Uniform Civil Code, and if its goal is to foster national unity with a "one nation-one people" slogan, or to abolish gender-based inequalities prevalent in all personal laws. These two goals are very distinct from one another. The Uniform Civil Code was first conceived as a way of encouraging national unification, with gender equality as a secondary goal. On the other hand, it has emerged as a champion of gender equality in recent times. The logic for this is that we have now realised that achieving some degree of equality among the public is vital in order to achieve a certain amount of "success," as some like to term it.

Gender equality is undeniably relevant and one of the most pressing topics of our day. Codification of sporadic laws and legal norms, religious decrees, customs, and cultural laws gives rules definitive status and simplifies law implementation. Such laws and regulations are likewise properly recognised and traceable for the rights and duties that result. The ultimate goal is a single system that controls the entire people equally and consistently and society is getting closer to that goal.

Uniform Civil Code is very important since it would provide equal rights to women in India, especially when religion-based personal laws are misogynistic. Women need to be put on the same pedestal as men. Uniform Civil Code holds within itself a power to materialise the same. Acceptance of this Code as a step towards gender equality should be encouraged. Both religious and personal laws should be assessed for implementation, and the best components from all major faiths as well as personal laws from other countries should be gathered and implemented.

Endnotes

1. Maithreyi Krishnaraj, "Women and the Public Domain: Critical Issues for Women Studies", Economic and Political Weekly 33 (1998), p. 393

2. Menski, Werner, "Modern Indian Family Law", online edn, Oxford Academic, Delhi, 2006

3. Yüksel Sezgin, "How to Integrate Universal Human Rights into Customary and Religious Legal Systems?", The Journal of Legal Pluralism and Unofficial Law 42 (2010), p. 5

4. Flavia Agnes, "Family Law Volume I: Family Laws and Constitutional Claims", New Delhi 2011, p.171

5. Subramanian, Narendra. *Nation and Family: Personal Law, Cultural Pluralism, and Gendered Citizenship in India*. 1st ed., Stanford University Press, 2014. *JSTOR*

6. Narain, Vrinda. *"Gender and Community: Muslim Women's Rights in India"*. University of Toronto Press, 2001. *JSTOR*.

7. Sathe, S. P. "Law and Women." *Economic and Political Weekly*, vol. 31, no. 41/42, 1996, pp. 2804–06. *JSTOR*.

8. Nandita Haksar "Human Rights Layering: A Feminist Perspective" in Amita Dhanda and Archana Parasher eds., Engendering Law. Essays in Honour of Lotika Sarkar Eastern Book Company, Lucknow, 1999

9. Supra note 6.

10. Rochana Bajpai, "Debating Difference: Group Rights and Liberal Democracy in India", New Delhi 2011, p. 183

11. Archana Parashar, "Women and Family Law Reform in India: Uniform Civil Code and Gender Equality", New Delhi 1992, p. 62

12. Werner Menski, "Hindu Law: Beyond Tradition and Modernity, New Delhi 2003, p. 161.

13. Siobhan Mullally, "Feminism and Multicultural Dilemmas in India", Oxford Journal of Legal Studies 24 (2004), p. 696.

14. Parashar, Archana. "Gender Inequality and Religious Personal Laws in India." *The Brown Journal of World Affairs*, vol. 14, no. 2, 2008, pp. 103–12. JSTOR.

15. J. Duncan M. Derrett, "Hindu Law, Past and Present", Calcutta 1957

16. Granville Austin, "Religion, Personal Law, and Identity in India", in: Gerald James Larson (ed.), 'Religion and Personal Law in Secular India: A Call to Judgment', Bloomington 2001, p. 18

17. John H. Mansfield, "The Personal Laws or a Uniform Civil Code?", in: Robert D. Baird (ed.), Independent India, New Delhi 2005.

18. Robert D. Baird, "Religion and Law in India: Adjusting to the Sacred as Secular", Independent India, New Delhi 2005, pp. 14-21

19. Nivedita Menon, "Seeing Like a Feminist", New Delhi 2012, p. 161.

20. Archana Parashar, "Just Family Law: Basic to all Indian Women", Common Law and Culture in South Asia, New Delhi 2005.

21. Parashar, Archana. "Gender Inequality and Religious Personal Laws in India." *The Brown Journal of World Affairs*, vol. 14, no. 2, 2008, pp. 103–12. JSTOR.

22. Bhattacharjee, Mahua. "WOMEN AND LAW: A GENDER PERSPECTIVE." *Proceedings of the Indian History Congress*, vol. 77, 2016, pp. 1054–58. JSTOR.

23. Crenshaw, "Demarginalizing the Intersection of Race and Sex: A Black Feminist Critique of Antidiscrimination Doctrine, Feminist Theory and Antiracist Politics." Chicago Legal Forum, 1989.

24. Dhanda, Amita. Review of WOMEN AND LAW IN INDIA. An Omnibus comprising of Flavia Agnes' "Law and Gender Inequality"; Sudhir Chandra's "Enslaved Daughters" and Monmayee Basu's "Hindu Women and Marriage Law"" *Journal of the Indian Law Institute*, vol. 49, no. 3, 2007, pp. 429–35. *JSTOR*.

CHAPTER 9

The Wise Are With the UCC

The constitution of India, the suprema Lex, is enacted in such a manner that it mirrors the qualities of the Indian social fabric. The essential fundamental principles, which form the core of the constitution, mirror the already existing social qualities of India as a society. Similarly, the Directive Principles, set the aspirations that are needed to be achieved in the long run. The state government bases its laws and programmes on the Directive Principles of State Policy, which have the goal of establishing a social and economic democracy. The constitution strikes a delicate balance between the rights and interests of an individual to practise religion and developing social harmony among the citizens. Article 44 of the Constitution expresses the idea of a uniform civil code for the citizens.

Steering the debate:

We keep seeing the seasonal debates over the Uniform Civil Code on different mediums, where several factions of society, in accordance with their own vested interests, keep raising the debate. These debates often start with highlighting the need for a uniform code or how it would destroy the homogeneous fabric of Indian society and gradually escalate to all the reasons that suit the vested and inherent interests of the parties to the debate. However, all the prime and vital reasons for demanding a robust, uniform civil code tend to seep through these agenda driven debates. Additionally, the ambiguous ideologies among the citizens also halt the process of enacting a uniform civil code.

A Universal Civil Code seeks to replace the various personal laws with a uniform set of laws that apply to all citizens of the nation. Due to the diversity of religion and community in the country of India, it again becomes a humongous task to deal with the personal matters of citizens under a single guise of legislature. This concept has received a myriad of responses and still continues to spark debates. The personal laws enacted by the colonial rulers have proved to be inconsistent and discriminatory from time to time. The issues regarding parity in inheritance rights for women, guardianship, interfaith marriages, and variation in the rights offered by these personal laws to different genders, are seldomly discussed in depth. Justice Arun Mishra, Chairperson of National Human Rights Commission stated,

"We see discrimination against women worldwide due to social, customary, and religious practises. The time has come to take care of same by enacting legislative provisions to remove discrimination in inheritance, property rights, parental rights, domicile of married women, and legal capacity."

Broadening his opinions, he further stated that, "Article 44 of the Constitution enabling equality by enacting a common civil code should not remain a dead letter" [1]. Nevertheless, his opinion is still currently residing in just the words, as these long running debates in the televisions and endless meetings are not resulting in a new ordinance.

India being a diverse nation, always have the diverse opinion from different religions and communities and the application of Uniform Civil Code will invite difference of opinions. The orthodox faction of the religious communities counters the need of such code by raising their right to practise the religion and its practises of their own choice. It is contended that such law would perforate the harmonious milieu of the country and disrupt the diverse social fabric. Similar claims were raised during constitutional debates, to which

Dr. BR Ambedkar had responded that "There was nothing new about the Uniform Civil Code. There already existed a common civil code in the country except for the areas of marriage, inheritance — which are the main targets for the Uniform Civil Code in the Draft Constitution." [2] The views of the founding father on the issue of implementing the code were very self-sufficient.

While hearing petitions on registration of interfaith marriages, Allahabad High Court explicitly brought to the fore the burning need of Uniform Civil Code and asked the government to work towards the direction of implementing the mandate of article 44. Justice Suneet Kumar stated that, "A common civil code will help the cause of national integration by removing disparate loyalties to laws that have conflicting ideologies" [3]

The Indian state of Goa is a shining example where the Indian government successfully proved the implementation of Uniform Civil Code. Concisely, Uniform Civil Code (UCC) is brought for one regulatory law for Indian states which would be pertinent to all religious and personal issues.

Cleofato Almeida Coutinho, a lawyer and a former member of Goa Law Commission propounded that, *"The Goa Civil Code is in force since Portuguese times and is considered a Uniform Civil Code. The provisions in the matter of succession are progressive to a large extent. And while when it comes to marriage and adoption, there is not complete uniformity, generally it is far more gender-just than other laws in the country".* [4]

The current scenario regarding the issues of religious and personal laws is resolved by the personal law boards and their existing provisions. For a nation like India, where peoples from different ethnicity, religion, and community reside together it becomes prominent to treat them equally in all forms. Observing the importance of a Uniform Civil Code, the Supreme Court in its landmark judgment of Shah Bano propounded that, "A common Civil Code will help the cause of national integration by removing disparate loyalties to laws which have conflicting ideologies."

With diversity in every aspect, India needs a uniform law or regulation that can equally serve each individual in same pedestal. All in all, the main objective of the Uniform Civil Code is to promote uniformity not only in the arena of religion and personal laws but also in the aspects of women and religious minorities. The complex laws of marriage, inheritance, divorce, succession, etc. will be resolved by one single regulation. At present, these issues are resolved by the personal laws and acts of every religion and community. India is currently dealing with several personal issues of religious affairs along with religious minority affairs. The violation and abuse of human rights law related to religious and communal affairs will be halted and permanently stopped with a uniform law.

A draft of the 'Progressive Uniform Civil Code' currently known as the Uniform Civil Code was presented to the then Chairman of the Law Commission, Justice BS Chauhan (Retd.) along with the contributing members consisting of eight eminent citizens, scholars, a retired senior Army officer, two Magsaysay award winners, writers, classical singer, and a legal luminary. [5] This difference in the committee proved lucrative as the ideas and concerns of various policymakers, scholars and activists can bring forth different issues from different corners of the communities including sexuality groups, concerns of different genders, and family life.

For many years, legislators have been engaged in discussions regarding enacting and implementing a Uniform Civil Code. Various political groups and interested parties have various opinions about the enactment of a uniform civil code. Diverse viewpoints and ideas have been expressed during Lok Sabha discussions of the Uniform Civil Code. Depending on their ideological leanings, different governments have adopted various positions on this topic. A variety of legal and constitutional factors, as well as the majority views in the Lok Sabha and Rajya Sabha, must all be taken into account before any legislation pertaining to the Uniform Civil Code is passed. To ensure that the aforementioned law is not mere a dead letter, it must be passed after extensive scrutiny by both the houses.

In the year 2018, a private member bill was introduced in Lok Sabha by Chandrakant Bhaurao Khaire Shri by the name of 'The Uniform Civil Code in India Bill, 2018' [6]. This private member bill was introduced with the main focus on the constitution of the National Inspection and Investigation Committee to prepare for the Uniform Civil Code along with its implementation throughout the territory of India.

In the year 2021, again, a private member bill was introduced in the lower house of the parliament by member Krupal Balaji Tumane Shri, by the name of 'The Uniform Civil Code Bill, 2019' [7]. Recently, The Uniform Civil Code Bill, 2021, a private member bill, introduced by Sushil Kumar Singh Shri in the Lok Sabha, has been a hot topic of debate in the prime time shows. [8] It is often claimed that the reason of successive introduction of these private member bills on UCC is for keeping the debate alive until the push comes to shove.

In the year 2022, a private member bill was introduced by Kirodi Lal Meena, a BJP member, which met with huge hue and cry from the members of opposition. The bill was vehemently and vociferously opposed by the members in opposition. It was also argued that passing of such a bill, will damage the secular fabric of the country and it must be withdrawn with an immediate effect. According to the bill, the National Inspection and Investigation Committee is to be established as part of the UCC planning and implementation process in India. The introduction of the bill was defended by the Union Minister Piyush Goyal, who stated that [9],

"Am pained to see the comments made by members quoting (B.R) Ambedkar. It is the legitimate right of a member to raise an issue which is under the directive principles of the constitution, let this subject be debated in the House. My colleague Prakash Javadekar will elaborate on this later but at this stage to cast aspersions on the government, to try to criticise the bill at introduction stage is uncalled for, I would like that the bill be introduced," [10]

However, these bills raise the complex issue of systematic implementation of UCC with a nationwide effect. In addition to these private member bills, government of Gujarat and Uttarakhand have progressed in the forming separate committees to work for the implementation and introduction of Uniform Civil Code. [11] Vices prevalent in the personal laws are not hidden, yet a blind is turned in the name of religion, whenever issue of parity in the personal laws is raised. It can be said that there is a collective lack of will, however, many states, on their own fiat had taken the matter into their own hands. Last year, Chief Minister of Assam, Hemant Biswa Sharma had stated that, "If Uniform Civil Code does not get implemented, the polygamy system will continue. A man will marry 3-4 times, curtailing the fundamental rights of a woman. Uniform Civil Code should be implemented for the greater interest of our Muslim women" [12] Owning to the importance of the issue, Union Law Minister Kiren Rijiju said in Parliament this year that the government currently had no plans to set up a panel to implement the UCC and requested the 22nd Law Commission of India to undertake an examination of various issues relating to the same. [13]

Apart from the arguments raised and claims made from the extreme ends of this debate, there are very few who provides a moderately balanced argument. One such argument has been put forth by Gautam Bhatia where he states,

"If there is a baseline consensus — grounded in the Constitution — of what constitutes gender equality and

fairness to women, it is clear that the additional goal of "uniformity" serves no intrinsic purpose. Prima facie, as long as personal laws are not violating anyone's rights, and treating everyone with equal concern and respect, there is no particular reason why — in a country as diverse and plural as India — people should not be given the opportunity to opt in or opt out of those regimes: In other words, if a person is free to choose whether they want to be governed by personal law, or by a non-religious civil code, there is no reason why UCC and personal laws cannot co-exist, instead of one replacing the other. Indeed, we already have an example of this: People who do not wish to marry under personal laws can marry under the Special Marriage Act (albeit not without problems and inconveniences)."

However, it would be impossible for an individual to choose from, if the second option is not yet in existence.

Celebrated jurist Tahir Mahmood expressed his opinion stating that the implementation of the common code must be nationwide and along with it all the regressive laws related to the personal laws must be abolished. In a piece written by him, he had very vocally mentioned his opinions on implementation of Uniform Civil Code in Indian scenario. He stated,

"Continued application of anachronistic foreign laws to Indian citizens in certain parts of the country stares in

the face of the constitutional goal of a UCC. Supposing that such a code can be enacted at the state-level, a beginning should be made by repealing and replacing them with the central marriage and succession laws in force everywhere else in the country. Taking this rational step should pose no problem as Goa is under the rule of the party in power at the Centre and Daman, Diu and Puducherry (as Union Territories) are also within its jurisdiction. Enforcing central family laws in these places will be all the more logical in view of the fact that in 2019, the government did extend them to Jammu, Kashmir and Ladakh, to replace their local variants — though unlike the Portuguese and French laws, they were neither of foreign origin nor antiquated." [14]

Union Minister Arun Jaitley, the then finance minister of the country, while opposing the party in opposition, emphasized that religion can't direct upon the rights and privileges of an individual conferred to it by the constitution and went after Congress over its stand on the Uniform Common Code, saying it was the Constituent assembly constrained by the party that had visualized a uniform civil law for all Indians.

"The Constitution today guarantees each individual right to equality, right to live with dignity. Therefore, as far as personal laws are concerned, I am one of those who believe that set of rights that personal law has... will have to be regulated by the Constitution." [15] The then finance minister further added that,

"Personal law cannot practise, propagate discrimination; cannot allow a compromise with human dignity. Personal law and practises can certainly deal with religion, can dictate upon rituals. The religion cannot dictate upon rights of individuals." [16]

Founding fathers and mothers of the Constitution of India were substantially tilted towards the enactment of Uniform Code for personal laws and expressed their strong views during constituent assembly debates. Founding mothers Amrit Kaur and Hansa Mehta Composed notes of dissent against choices that consigned the uniform common code to the non-justiciable privileges, permitted the state to force enrolment for mandatory military assistance, at each stage when the advisory groups made their authority proposals to the higher bodies of the assembly.

Dr. B.R. Ambedkar, Chairman of the Drafting Committee, during the Constituent Assembly debates, had very vocally defended the idea of Uniform Civil Code. He along with several other doyens of law, was a supporter of Uniform Civil Court and its implementation. During his speeches, while putting his views to the fore, he highlighted the evident dissent that this idea may face during its implementation. He had stated that,

"I personally do not understand why religion should be given this vast, expansive jurisdiction so as to cover the whole of life and to prevent the legislature from encroaching upon that field. After all, what are we having this liberty for?"

"We are having this liberty in order to reform our social system, which is so full of inequities, so full of inequalities, discriminations and other things, which conflict with our fundamental rights." No one need be apprehensive... that if the state has the power, the state will immediately proceed to execute... that power in a manner that may be found to be objectionable by the Muslims or by the Christians or by any other community...,"

"It does not say that after the Code is framed the State shall enforce it upon all citizens merely because they are citizens. It is perfectly possible that the future Parliament may make a provision by way of making a beginning that the Code shall apply only to those who make a declaration that they are prepared to be bound by it, so that in the initial stage the application of the Code may be purely voluntary,". [17]

In the landmark judgment of *Sarla Mudgal* [18], red-carpet treatment is due for Justice Kuldip Singh's unvarnished views, which demand and merit the implementation of Uniform Code. He said that by codifying the traditional Hindu Law (also known as Personal Law of the Hindus), which governs marriage, succession, and descent, it was made more enforceable. Delaying the implementation of unified personal law throughout the nation indefinitely has absolutely no rationale. [19]

The learned judge continued by noting that those who preferred to stay in India after partition were aware that Indian leaders did not subscribe to the idea of two or three nations, and that there would only be one nation—the Indian Nation—in the Indian Republic, with no community able to assert its independence on the basis of religion. [20]

Justice Kuldip Singh's observations are nothing but calling a spade a spade. Even a layperson, not only a lawman, might understand this decision. Along with the opinions of Hon'ble Justice Kuldip Singh, Hon'ble Justice Y.V. Chandrachud observed that, thus, we comprehend the challenges involved in bringing people of diverse religions and persuasions together on a same platform, the honourable judge said. But if the Constitution was to signify anything, a start had to be made.

The current imbalance in Indian laws and their feeble implementation is generating several different problems. For the same reason, this powerful shift in the implementation of the

Uniform Civil Code (UCC) wouldn't just help with resolving the communal issues but would also help in halting the gender-based oppression that will ultimately strengthen the Indian legislation.

Ultimately, all the debates surrounding the issue boil down to one issue, i.e., the constitutionality of the implementation of UCC, which has often been very minutely discussed in several public platforms. Here, it becomes crucial to state that negating UCC on the mere basis of it being a DPSP is as feeble as a sand castle on a seashore. It has been explicitly re-iterated that the harmony between the fundamental and DPSP is of the prime essence, not the superiority of one over the other. It should be considered that the DPSP are fundamental to governance, and it shall be the duty of the state to implement them through laws and statutes.

Since directive principles lay down the humanitarian and socialistic precepts of Indian society and aim to bring about a social revolution in Indian society, it is high time that a well-researched law on the issue be introduced into the governance and implemented with nationwide effect. This well researched law should cover every single aspect of religious communities that is most disputed and contributes to the majority of cases.

It is pertinent for this new code to deal with the communities that are usually not considered or looked at in different religions. The LGBTQ community, along with the transgenders, gays, and bisexuals, are usually found quarrelling and altercating with the government for their rights. For the same, the major change proposed is to give lesbian, gay, bisexual, queer (LGBTQ), and transgender people equivalent privileges to marry according to their choices, to adopt children, to use simplified divorce procedures, and to share in the inheritance of property.

This article came to be passed after significant discussion by the authorities. Also, the people who participated in the discussion and contributed to this article were never marked as communal, even by the staunchest communalists. For pointless reasons, unreasonable contentions were being advanced questioning the fruitful execution of this directive principle. [21]

Notes

1. Awstika Das, Uniform Civil Code Necessary, Discrimination Against Women In Personal Laws Should Be Removed: NHRC Chairperson Justice Arun Mishra, LIVE LAW (Dec. 10, 2022, 03:46 P.M.) https://www.livelaw.in/top-stories/uniform-civil-code-necessary-discrimination-against-women-in-personal-laws-should-be-removed-nhrc-chairperson-justice-arun-mishra-216339#:~:text=Article%2044%20of%20the%20Constitution,Human%20Rights%20Commission%2C%20Arun%20Mishra

2. *Ambedkar and Uniform Civil Code. Why Ambedkar supported Uniform Civil Code*, THE HINDU BUSINESS LINE (April 14, 2021) https://www.thehindubusinessline.com/opinion/why-ambedkar-supported-uniform-civil-code/article34320070.ece

3. Writ No. 14896 of 2021.

4. Gerard De Souza, *The Goa civil code, the new model for a uniform civil code*, HINDUSTAN TIMES (May 12, 2022, 2:55 A.M.) https://www.hindustantimes.com/india-news/explained-the-goa-civil-code-the-new-model-for-a-uniform-civil-code-101652304333768.html

5. Seema Chishti, *Uniform Civil Code draft handed over to law panel chief*, INDIAN EXPRESS (Oct. 12, 2017, 02:19 A.M.) https://indianexpress.com/article/india/uniform-civil-code-draft-handed-over-to-law-panel-chief-4885969/

6. Bill produced in the Parliament, available at: https://loksabha.nic.in/Legislation/billintroduce.aspx

7. Ibid

8. Ibid

9. Vijaita Singh, *BJP member moves private member bill on Uniform Civil Code in Rajya Sabha, draws stiff resistance from opposition*, THE HINDU (Dec. 09, 2022, 04:28 P.M.), https://www.thehindu.com/news/national/private-members-bill-on-uniform-civil-code-introduced-in-rajya-sabha/article66242700.ece

10. Id.

11. Saubhadra Chatterji & Smriti Kak Ramachandran, *Private Bill for UCC listed for upcoming session*, HINDUSTAN TIMES (Jan. 25, 2023, 1:49 A.M.) https://www.hindustantimes.com/india-news/private-bill-on-ucc-listed-for-upcoming-session-101674585364892.html

12. *Assam CM calls for implementation of Uniform Civil Code to stop polygamy*, BUSINESS STANDARD (May 1, 2022, 8:49 P.M.), https://www.business-standard.com/article/current-affairs/assam-cm-calls-for-implementation-of-uniform-civil-code-to-stop-polygamy-122050100818_1.html

13.] Diksha Munjal, *The Uniform Civil Code*, THE HINDU (Nov. 6, 2022, 10:54 P.M.), https://www.thehindu.com/news/national/explained-the-uniform-civil-code/article66105351.ece#:~:text=While%20the%20

UCC%20is%20a,issues%20relating%20to%20the%20same

14. Tahir Mahmood, "How to make a Uniform Civil Code", The Hindu, *available at:* https://indianexpress.com/article/opinion/columns/uniform-civil-code-states-level-ucc-7916033/

15. Religion can't dictate upon rights of individuals: Arun Jaitley, *available at:* https://economictimes.indiatimes.com/news/politics-and-nation/religion-cant-dictate-upon-rights-of-individuals-arun-jaitley/articleshow/54839187.cms?utm_source=contentofinterest&utm_medium=text&utm_campaign=cppst

16. Ibid.

17. Ambedkar favoured common civil code, However, he did not want it imposed on citizens by force, The Hindu, available at: https://www.thehindu.com/news/national/ambedkar-favoured-common-civil-code/article7934565.ece

18. Sarla Mudgal, President, Kalyani v. Union of India, (1995) 3 SCC 635.

19. Ibid.

20. Ibid.

21. LALRINAWMI RALTE & STELLA FARIA, WAGING PEACE: BUILDING A WORLD IN WHICH LIFE MATTERS [Indian Women in Theology (IWIT)/ISPCK, 2004].

CHAPTER 10

The Way Forward

The issue of implementation of a uniform code of Civil nature has been laid down categorically in the chapters before. After coming this far, it becomes essential to synthesize your thoughts and see the entire issue with a vantage point of *need and desirability.* The real essence of this book, is to present this crucial issue and its various dimensions. However, it should be kept in mind that though this issue has faced staunch opposition, its importance is still persisting amidst the tyrannical personal laws.

The historical background of UCC in India reveals a complex and contentious journey. The idea of a UCC dates back to the colonial era when the British sought to implement uniform laws to govern their diverse subjects. However, due to various political and religious considerations, the issue of implementing a UCC in independent India became highly controversial. India's Constitution, adopted in 1950, recognized the importance of maintaining personal laws based on religious beliefs to accommodate its diverse population. Consequently, Article 44 of the Constitution aimed to secure a UCC for all citizens, but its implementation has remained a subject of intense debate and resistance.

Over the years, several attempts have been made to bring about a UCC, but they have encountered strong opposition from religious and conservative groups who argue for the preservation of religious personal laws. These groups believe that personal laws are an integral part of their religious identity and any attempts to enforce a uniform code would infringe upon their religious freedom.

The Indian judiciary has also played a significant role in shaping the discourse around the UCC. Several landmark judgments, such as the Shah Bano case in 1985, sparked debates on the need for a uniform code to ensure gender justice and equality. However, the fear of religious backlash and political expediency have often hindered substantial progress towards a UCC. It is essential to acknowledge that the UCC debate goes beyond legal and constitutional considerations. It is a reflection of the broader socio-political landscape of India, where identity politics and communal tensions play a crucial role. Any attempt to implement a UCC must navigate these complex dynamics while ensuring inclusivity, social cohesion, and respect for religious beliefs.

The historical background of the UCC in India demonstrates the deep-rooted complexities and challenges involved in realizing a uniform civil code. While the idea of a UCC remains a matter of debate and contention, any future endeavors must strike a delicate balance between individual rights, religious freedom, and the principles of justice and equality. Only through open dialogue, consensus-building, and a commitment to secularism can a meaningful and inclusive UCC be envisioned and implemented in India.

Further, the debates within the Constituent Assembly of India regarding the UCC were suggestive of the complex challenges faced in reconciling diverse religious and cultural practices with the vision of a unified legal framework for all citizens. During the framing of the Indian Constitution, there were spirited discussions on the need for a UCC to promote equality, justice, and secularism. Proponents argued that a UCC would ensure gender justice, protect individual rights, and foster national integration. They believed that personal laws based on religious practices perpetuated discrimination and hindered social progress. However, opponents expressed concerns about the potential erosion of religious freedom and the preservation of cultural identities. They emphasized the importance of maintaining personal laws that were deeply intertwined with religious practices and traditions. The fear of alienating religious communities and disrupting social harmony became a key factor in the debates.

The framers of the Constitution recognized the sensitivities surrounding the UCC issue and sought a middle ground. Article 44 of the Constitution was included as a directive principle, encouraging the state to strive towards enacting a UCC while respecting existing personal laws. This reflected a pragmatic approach that sought to balance competing interests. The debates in the Constituent Assembly underscored the significance of accommodating diversity while striving for social reform and justice. The framers recognized that a one-size-fits-all approach might not be immediately feasible in a country as pluralistic as India. They acknowledged the need for gradual and consensual reforms that considered the social, cultural, and religious realities of the nation. The debates also highlighted the limitations of the Constitution as a transformative document. While the Constitution laid the groundwork for a UCC, it did not provide a definitive solution, leaving the matter open to future legislation and interpretation by the judiciary.

The debates within the Constituent Assembly on the UCC reflected the nuanced considerations and challenges faced in the quest for a unified legal framework. The framers recognized the importance of individual rights, religious freedom, and cultural preservation, while simultaneously advocating for social reform and gender justice. The Constitution's directive principles provided a roadmap for future endeavors, emphasizing the need for gradual progress and consensus-building. Ultimately, the debates laid the foundation for ongoing discussions and legal interpretations regarding the UCC in India.

The implementation of UCC in India has been influenced by the contributions of various key stakeholders who have advocated for its realization, albeit with differing perspectives and motivations. One of the significant contributors to the implementation of a UCC has been the judiciary. Over the years, the Indian courts have delivered landmark judgments that highlighted the need for a UCC to ensure gender justice, equality, and the protection of fundamental rights. These judgments, such as the Shah Bano case, have sparked debates and pushed for a reexamination of personal laws.

Another crucial contributor to the UCC's implementation has been progressive thinkers, activists, and organizations. These individuals and groups have tirelessly campaigned for a unified legal framework, highlighting the discriminatory aspects of existing personal laws and advocating for equal rights for all citizens. They have championed gender justice, individual freedom, and the principles of secularism as the basis for a UCC. Additionally, scholars, academics, and legal experts have made significant contributions through their research, analysis, and intellectual discourse. Their writings and discussions have helped shape the understanding of the UCC and its potential impact on society. They have provided insights into the legal, social, and cultural dimensions of implementing a UCC, paving the way for informed debates and discussions. Politicians and policymakers have also played a crucial role in the implementation of a UCC. While political will and consensus have been challenging to achieve, some leaders have advocated for the need to move towards a UCC, highlighting its benefits in terms of national integration, social harmony, and gender equality. Their efforts in raising awareness, initiating legislative discussions, and proposing reforms have contributed to keeping the UCC on the national agenda.

The quest for the implementation of a UCC in India has benefited from the contributions of various key stakeholders. The judiciary, progressive thinkers, activists, scholars, politicians, and policymakers have all played significant roles in advocating for the UCC, each bringing unique perspectives and motivations to the table. While challenges and differences of opinion persist, their collective efforts have kept the discourse alive and have helped shape the understanding and potential implementation of a UCC in India.

In India, the court will play a crucial role in installing the Uniform Civil Code (UCC) into effect. In order to provide justice and equality for all people, the court plays a critical role as an institution in the interpretation and application of the law. The lords of the law had repeatedly emphasised the need to put into effect the Uniform Civil Code on several occasions. When we take into account a few decided cases, the judiciary has declared its support for the formulation of the Uniform Civil Code in consonance with Article 44 of the Constitution. The Court's position on adopting a universal civil code is based on the notion that such a code will help to create a sense national cooperation and integrity as well as safeguarding those who are oppressed by the conduct of others. The judiciary has frequently stepped in to address the injustices brought on by tyranny disguised as personal laws. If the verdict, however, didn't live up to the political aspirations of the ruling party, it was reversed by passing laws that negated the judgment's impact. The courts have not decided how proportionately this uniform code would be applied to different groups. Each community will need to give these laws a great deal of thought and discussion before they can be codified. There will be opposition to its implementation from some social groups, but this should not be an excuse to drag out the process for longer than necessary. In light of the constitutional obligation, the current administration should move quickly.

The judiciary can actively encourage and entertain PILs related to the implementation of a UCC. PILs allow citizens to bring matters of public importance to the court's attention, and the judiciary can utilize this tool to address specific issues and ensure that the implementation of a UCC is in the public interest. In addition to it, hon'ble judicial institutions can engage in judicial activism by taking suo moto cognizance of cases or issues related to personal laws and religious practices that hinder the implementation of a UCC. By proactively addressing these issues, the judiciary can promote a uniform legal framework and protect the rights of individuals. Most prominently, the judiciary can establish specific timelines for the legislature to enact laws related to the UCC. By providing a time-bound framework, the judiciary can exert pressure on the government and ensure that necessary steps are taken to implement a UCC within a reasonable period. The judiciary must strike a delicate balance between preserving personal freedoms and promoting a unified legal framework that upholds constitutional values. Hence, it can be concluded that the court plays a significant role in putting the Uniform Civil Code into effect. The court may aid in the realisation of a more just legal system that respects the rights and aspirations of all people, regardless of their religious or cultural connections, by interpreting the Constitution and rendering progressive judgements.

The global viewpoint on UCC offers a variety of ideas and perspectives. While a few nations have adopted it to encourage equality and secularism, others are opting to retain religious or customary rules for a variety of reasons. Adoption or rejection of the UCC is frequently affected by past, societal, and political circumstances unique to each country.

By establishing a standard set of laws for all citizens, irrespective of their religion or cultural background, supporters of UCC claim that it promotes social cohesiveness, gender equality, and individual liberties. They claim the fact that everyone is bound by the same set of laws minimizes bias, discrimination, and prejudices and fosters a sense of national belonging. Additionally, it can improve administrative effectiveness, streamline legal procedures, and lessen conflicts brought on by competing personal laws.

On the other hand, detractors worry that a single civil code could erode the self-determination and uniqueness of minority communities, raising concerns about the potential damage to cultural and religious diversity. They stress the significance of upholding and supporting each individual's right to practice their religion freely and to engage in cultural practices.

Recognizing that each nation's route toward the UCC is distinct and must be formed by its particular social, cultural, and political factors is vital. It is important to customize any prospective implementation of the UCC to the particular requirements and goals of the society in question by learning from international experiences that might offer insights and novel approaches. To ensure a thorough knowledge of the ramifications and to build an agreement on the best course of action, a meaningful and inclusive discourse including all stakeholders, including religious leaders, legal professionals, activists, and people, is essential.

Implementing a UCC can have several advantages that exceed the drawbacks. It can be considered as a move closer to a society that is more growing, open, and inclusive. It guarantees that all citizens, irrespective of their religious convictions, are dealt with equally and fairly before the law. By removing inequalities and exclusionary practices that may occur under personal laws based on religion, UCC advances the values of fairness and equity. The advancement of equality between genders is one of the UCC's other important benefits. Religiously based personal laws frequently have clauses that act unfairly against women in areas like marriage, divorce, inheritance, and child custody. By eradicating these unjust practices, a UCC can give women equal rights and opportunities. Promoting a feeling of a collective sense of self and beliefs among citizens, UCC also advances social cohesion. Different personal laws have a dividing effect, but UCC aids in bridging that gap while promoting harmony and cohesion within society. A UCC can help create a society that is more unified and accepting by treating all citizens equally.

Personalized rules based on religion can be confusing and challenging to understand, making them problematic from a legal standpoint. By establishing a single set of laws that apply to all citizens, a uniform civil code streamlines the legal system and makes it simpler for people to comprehend and exercise their rights. By streamlining the legal system, we can ensure that everyone understands their rights and obligations under the law. Finally, a UCC emphasizes individual rights and freedoms, which represents a progressive and contemporary attitude. It can assist in addressing regressive behaviors and harmonizing personal laws with current cultural norms. A UCC can support the overall growth and evolution of society by making sure that laws adapt to the times.

To put it plainly, the global viewpoint on UCC highlights the intricate interplay between the values of equality, cultural variety, and personal freedom. While some nations have adopted UCC to advance secularism and gender equity, others have chosen alternate strategies that consider religious and cultural diversity. To preserve individual rights while promoting a just and peaceful society, the choice to enact UCC should be made with consideration, inclusion, and a thorough awareness of the local environment. In order to guarantee that the code is equitable and preserves individual rights, it is imperative to take into account the varied cultural and religious views of the population. Addressing concerns and ensuring a seamless transition towards UCC require candid and open conversations and engagements with all parties.

The recommendations put forth by the Law Commission of India regarding the implementation of UCC are crucial steps toward achieving social and legal uniformity in the country. The commission's comprehensive analysis and proposed reforms aim to address the diverse personal laws prevailing in India and establish a common set of civil laws applicable to all citizens, irrespective of their religious affiliations. The recommendations emphasize the need for equality, non-discrimination, and gender justice. By advocating for a UCC, the commission seeks to promote a harmonious society where all individuals are granted equal rights and opportunities, regardless of their religious backgrounds. The proposed code aims to eliminate gender biases and discriminatory practices that exist within various personal laws, ensuring that women are treated on par with men in matters such as marriage, divorce, inheritance, and property rights.

Furthermore, the commission's recommendations strive to uphold the principles of secularism and national integration. A UCC would contribute to fostering a sense of unity and cohesion among diverse communities in India, as it would eliminate the perception of differential treatment based on religion. It would reinforce the idea of a secular state where all citizens are subject to the same laws and are equally protected under the legal system, regardless of their religious beliefs.

However, it is important to acknowledge that the implementation of a UCC should be approached with sensitivity and careful consideration of various socio-cultural factors. The commission's recommendations recognize the need for an inclusive and consultative process, involving stakeholders from different communities, to ensure that the proposed code reflects the aspirations and concerns of all citizens. Any implementation of a UCC should be done in a manner that respects religious diversity, safeguards minority rights, and accommodates the genuine concerns of different communities.

In conclusion, the Law Commission of India's recommendations on the implementation of UCC represent a significant step towards achieving legal uniformity, gender justice, and social cohesion. The proposed code, while aiming to uphold the principles of equality and secularism, should be implemented in a consultative and inclusive manner, taking into account the sensitivities and concerns of all communities. Through such a balanced approach, India can move towards a more equitable and unified society, where citizens enjoy equal rights and protections under a common civil law framework.

As a final observation and a direction for the discussion, it can be said that the said reforms are intended to make the laws more modern, progressive, and gender-neutral to keep up with the times. According to the Law Panel, when it concerns the execution of a UCC, it would be a practice where every rule and best practice from every faith are chosen and a unified code for reference is established. This practice will also help to foster trust among each community.

Yet, as it has been discussed, the biggest problem with the UCC has been its implementation, which is greatly influenced by several factors, including both social and political contexts, which will have differing opinions as to if a UCC is appealing or not. From the inception of the colonial period till the present, excellent considerations have been made both for and against the UCC. However, it can be inferred (from their report) that the UCC did not appeal to the Law panel and they considered its implementation would be infructuous as they believed, it is likely to fail at achieving the desired goals.

The author contends that the enactment of UCC should be given more weight if the Law Panel's arguments are to be examined from the standpoint of implementation because codification and standardization through a UCC would be the most optimal way to accomplish the same. The argument for a secular state and the right to practice one's religion does not need to be abandoned to implement a UCC because India will continue to be a secular nation with many diverse communities that will be subject to a single codified law while being free to practice their respective religions and customs. Therefore, such a code must be put in place to combat the known devil and be ready for any potential foes that could harm India's diversity.

India is home to more than 1.3 billion people, who come from a variety of linguistic, cultural, and religious origins. Religion and its wide variation are seen as one of the most significant barriers when it comes to the discussion of the Uniform Civil Code and its implementation in India. The subject matter here is based on religion because we are concerned that bringing uniformity to our religion and culture would destroy our sense of self and subsequently rob us of our right to practise religion. By encouraging a feeling of equality and fairness among all people, regardless of their faith, the Uniform Civil Code can be a useful instrument for resolving religious strife in India. The personal laws of different religions can be replaced with a uniform set of laws, ensuring that everyone is treated equally in areas like marriage, divorce, inheritance, and property rights while also ensuring that our right to practise religion under Article 25 is completely preserved. The terrible aspects of our religion are being eliminated, allowing for the adoption of better practises in other religions and this culmination occurs under the flag of the Uniform Civil Code. However, it is important to acknowledge that the path towards implementing a UCC that satisfies all religious communities is fraught with challenges. The deeply rooted religious beliefs, traditions, and social norms make it a contentious issue. It demands a comprehensive and inclusive approach that involves extensive consultations with religious leaders, scholars, and representatives from different communities to address concerns and build consensus. We cannot disregard the problems that India is now facing, particularly the enormous diversity of religious groups and their associated customs.

We must, though, take into account, the possible advantages of measures that can promote national unification, such as the adoption of a Uniform Civil Code. Discussions on this subject are essential because they help us spot problems and weaknesses and take steps towards a brighter future. Implementing a UCC requires navigating through these complexities and addressing concerns raised by various religious communities. It demands engaging in constructive dialogues and consultations to arrive at a consensus that respects the constitutional values of equality, justice, and non-discrimination while safeguarding religious freedom. Striking a balance between individual rights, equality, and religious freedom is no easy task. It requires a nuanced understanding of the cultural and religious sensitivities prevailing in the country. The implementation of a UCC must be approached with sensitivity and a commitment to preserving the pluralistic nature of Indian society.

The Chapter on the advantages of UCC provides how the implementation of a UCC holds the potential to pave a better future for India. While the subject of UCC has been a topic of debate and discussion for many years, it is essential to recognize the potential benefits it can bring to the country. First and foremost, the UCC promotes equality and justice by providing a common set of laws that apply to all citizens, irrespective of their religious or cultural background. This eliminates the existing disparities and ensures that all individuals are treated fairly under the law. It fosters a sense of unity and national identity, reinforcing the principle of a secular and inclusive India. Additionally, UCC can help in safeguarding the rights of individuals, particularly women. By harmonizing personal laws relating to marriage, divorce, inheritance, and adoption, it can eliminate discriminatory practices and empower women by granting them equal rights and protection. This not only enhances their social and economic status but also contributes to their overall well-being and development.

Furthermore, UCC simplifies the legal framework and enhances the efficiency of the judicial system. It reduces the complexity and confusion arising from the existence of multiple personal laws and ensures a more streamlined and consistent approach to legal matters. This can lead to quicker resolution of disputes and a more accessible and transparent legal system for all citizens. It is important to acknowledge that the implementation of UCC requires sensitivity, inclusiveness, and a thorough understanding of diverse religious and cultural practices. It should be approached with a willingness to engage in dialogue and consultation with all stakeholders to ensure that the concerns and interests of different communities are respected and addressed.

Simply put, the adoption of UCC in India has the potential to create a more harmonious, equitable, and progressive society. By upholding the principles of equality, justice, and inclusiveness, it can foster national unity, protect individual rights, and streamline the legal system. However, it is crucial to proceed with careful consideration, taking into account the diverse cultural and religious fabric of the nation. Through open and respectful dialogue, India can work towards a future where every citizen is treated with fairness and dignity, regardless of their background.

The chapter went into great detail about the need for a UCC in our nation for different reasons best discussed in the chapter. One of the key goals is to uphold the Indian Constitution's tenet of equality by making sure that everyone is subject to the same rules in private affairs like inheritance, adoption, marriage, and divorce, regardless of religion. The existing framework of personal laws, which is based on religious practices and conventions, frequently supports bias towards women and gender inequality.

By establishing a consistent civil code for all people of the nation, UCC would also aid in promoting national unification and unity. Removing the impression of distinct treatment of various religious communities would aid in creating societal cohesion and lowering intercommunity tensions. Additionally, the existence of many personal laws based on religious conventions and practices frequently causes confusion and conflict, particularly in situations involving interfaith marriages and succession. By offering an unequivocal legal foundation for resolution, the UCC would aid in settling such disputes.

The fundamental purpose of the UCC is to advocate for the eradication of all social ills, regardless of whether they are based on gender or religion. While attempting to resolve the current problems through the application of the UCC, we must focus on two areas in particular.

The first issue that comes up is how to maintain consistency in personal laws while still respecting local differences. It is crucial to assess whether we dismiss a community's customs as archaic and unfair without giving them considerable thought. We risk making the same mistake as the Americans, who viewed the native population as barbarians in need of saving by the forward-looking, civilized standards of Christianity, if we fail to tackle these issues. The second concern is whether standardization has been successful in eradicating gender disparities that still lower women's standing in our society. The previous query is connected to this one. It is crucial to recognize the many levels of gender disparities and injustices that exist across each society because the concept of inequality may change from one group to the next. A community's regulations may have provisions that go counter to the idea of equal status for women in that society. Therefore, eradicating these unfair practices that are specific to that group should be the first step. It is essential for each community to first recognize the meanings of inequality and injustice within their sector of existence rather than hurriedly coming up with an all-encompassing description of injustice and inequality, which is the prevalent point of view. Otherwise, groups may become protective in response to calls for conformity, which could lead to injustices within such groups.

While striving to make our society more effective, we must be mindful that progress is a gradual process and that not every aspect of life can be sped up. These repeated requests for UCC can serve as an alarm for us to reform the personal law system as needed and concentrate on finding solutions to the problems. The original purpose of the Uniform Civil Code was to promote national unification, with gender equality as a secondary objective. On the other side, the Uniform Civil Code has lately been a champion of gender equality. The justification for this is that we now understand how important it is to attain a certain level of equality among the populace in order to achieve a particular level of "success," as some like to call it.

If we classify the era of the struggle of the women in the society, the contemporary times can be regarded as the time where women are nudging their way to the front, it can be termed as the era of assertion, assertion of their bodily autonomy, rights concerning them and many more things. In this context, this topic of viewing the crucial concept of implementation of a uniform Civil Code in the country with a vantage point of women, makes this chapter, the most intriguing of all. the implementation of a Uniform Civil Code (UCC) in India holds several benefits for women, fostering gender equality and empowering them in various aspects of their lives. The current scenario of personal laws in India, which vary based on religious affiliations, often perpetuates discriminatory practices, and denies women their fundamental rights. By adopting a UCC, the country can address these disparities and provide a more equitable legal framework for women. Currently, personal laws often place women at a disadvantage when it comes to matters such as marriage, divorce, inheritance, and child custody. A UCC would ensure that women are treated on an equal footing with men, irrespective of their religious background. It would eliminate discriminatory practices and provide women with equal rights and opportunities, enhancing their social, economic, and personal well-being.

Implementation of the uniform code will ensure that the golden *right of choice* is bestowed to the women in the country who are often cornered down due to different religious and personal laws. What took a catena of judgements, social movements, and massive uproar to equalise the grounds of rights between the sexes, can be done by a single code of civil laws. Additionally, such code would simplify legal procedures and ensure consistent and efficient administration of justice. The current fragmented system, with different sets of laws for different religious communities, often leads to confusion and delays in resolving disputes. By establishing a uniform legal code, women would have greater clarity and access to justice, enabling them to seek remedies promptly and effectively. It is crucial to understand that complete social changes, awareness campaigns, and sensitization initiatives should go hand in hand with the implementation of a UCC. The government, courts, civil society organisations, and religious leaders must all work together to change deeply rooted social attitudes and practises. A UCC may be implemented successfully, ensuring that its advantages are felt by women across the nation, by engaging in debate, resolving concerns, and encouraging knowledge.

The wise men who have carefully examined the issue strongly advocate for the implementation of a Uniform Civil Code (UCC) in India. Their support stems from several compelling reasons rooted in fairness, equality, and societal progress. First and foremost, a UCC would ensure that all citizens, irrespective of their religious affiliations, are subject to the same set of laws. This uniformity in the legal framework is seen as a cornerstone of a just and egalitarian society. Wise men argue that treating individuals differently based on their religious background perpetuates inequality and hampers national integration. By embracing a UCC, India would take a significant step towards fostering unity, solidarity, and social cohesion among its diverse populace.

Furthermore, proponents of a UCC contend that it would eliminate the prevailing disparities and discriminatory practices against women entrenched in personal laws. These laws, influenced by religious traditions, often deny women their fundamental rights in areas such as marriage, divorce, inheritance, and child custody. Wise men emphasize the need to uphold gender equality and empower women by providing them with equal rights and opportunities under a uniform legal code. They believe that a UCC would be a significant stride towards dismantling the archaic norms that hinder women's progress and autonomy.

The wise men also argue that a UCC would simplify and expedite legal processes, ensuring greater efficiency and accessibility to justice. The current system, with multiple sets of laws based on religious communities, leads to confusion and delays in resolving disputes. By establishing a single legal framework, a UCC would streamline legal proceedings, making them more transparent, equitable, and responsive to the needs of citizens. Moreover, the prudent men assert that a UCC would for catalyze societal progress and modernization. It would challenge regressive customs and practices prevalent in certain personal laws, fostering a more inclusive and forward-thinking society. By promoting individual freedoms and ensuring equal rights for all, a UCC would enable citizens to participate fully in social, economic, and cultural spheres, thereby contributing to the overall development of the nation. The introduction of a Uniform Civil Code in India is strongly backed by wise men because it to cancan promote harmony, protect gender equality, simplify legal processes, and advance society. They contend that adopting a UCC puts India on a path towards a society where there is greater harmony and equity and is consistent with the values of justice, equality, and national integration.

At the end of this work, I would like to leave the readers with a riveting thought, that has resonated by one of our founding mothers of the Constitution of India, *'Not only have custom and usage dealt harshly with us, but even the law has militated and continues to militate against us'*. It has now become the dire need and a state responsibility to regulate the laws and present a uniform Civil code for a unified nation.

About The Author

Author is an Advocate, joined this noble profession in the year 2008 and since then he has sincerely made various efforts for the welfare of the legal fraternity.

He is grand-son of Late Dr. Dhan Prakash Gupta, who joined this noble profession in 1961 and was a prominent advocate from Delhi. He was a Member of Bar Council of Delhi and was also the Chairman of Disciplinary and Enrolment Committee. He is known for providing biggest Library, through his office, to the young lawyers who used to often visit his office as it was open to all.

Dr. D. P. Gupta's contribution to the society is evident from his writings in the form of almost 20 books that have been published, which include historic work of translation and transliteration of the "holy Quran" titled as "Pavitra Quran Darshan". He was also honored and was conferred with various awards namely "Sahitya Samman, Madan Mohan Malviye Ji Award, Kavya Gaurav Award and was also awarded Gyanacharya by the Kabir Panthi Mahasabha". At a very early age of 62 years Dr. Gupta decided to stop working for financial gains, and spent later of his life for social causes and also donated well-furnished "Bar Room" for lady advocates.

Author's grand-father Dr. Dhan Prakash Gupta Left his legacy which is being nurtured by his father Mr. Anil Kumar Gupta, who is an equally prominent lawyer and a former Vice President of Delhi Bar Association. He is the one who introduced the concept of lawyer's Welfare Stamp during his tenure of Vice President, Delhi Bar Association (1992-1994).

Thereafter, the author being the eldest son in the family also joined this profession in the year 2008 and followed all the steps taught by his late grand- father and his father for the welfare of this fraternity.

His family has devoted more than 60 years for the development of the legal fraternity and have always been dedicated to maintain the sanctity of the legal profession and left no stone unturned to uplift the status of lawyer's fraternity.

Author is an Elected Member of the Bar Council of Delhi since 2018, and then became youngest Co-Chairman, BCD. In May 2021, He was appointed as Hony. Secretary, Bar Council of Delhi for a short period till July 2021. During the entire tenure he tried his best and taken all initiative for betterment of legal fraternity including few very important steps taken during COVID First and Second Wave wherein Bar Council of Delhi has provided following type of assistance to the advocates;

1. Financial assistance of Rs.5000 each to around 18,300 advocates.

2. 15,000/- each to around 5000 advocates who got infected with Corona and were Home Quarantine.

3. 50,000/- each to around 70 advocates who were hospitalised due to Covid-19.

4. Ration kits to 3000 advocates and further tie up with Patanjali wherein prepaid groceries card worth

Rs.2000/- each were provided to around 10,000 advocates.

5. 110 Oxygen cylinders have been purchased which is being regularly circulated between lawyers who were in need of the same.

Total around rupees 21 Crore have been disbursed till date for the benefit of the lawyers.

In April 2023, first ever National Lawyers Parliament Festival was organised by the efforts of author, which witnesses heated debates on the issue of Uniform Civil Code.

Apart from above, Author is also associated with few other associations and organisations including;

President, Bharat Uday Foundation

President, National Association of Democratic Lawyers

Founder Trustee, Lawyers for Justice.

Member, Rotary Club of Delhi Midwest

Member, Lions Club Trans Yamuna

Member, Masonic Club, Tolstoy Road, Janpath, Delhi

Joint Secretary, Sant Vivekananda Educational and Welfare Society running its Law College namely "Sant Vivekananda College of Law and Higher Studies" at Ghaziabad but affiliated from GGSIP University, Delhi.

www.ingramcontent.com/pod-product-compliance
Lightning Source LLC
LaVergne TN
LVHW010312070526
838199LV00065B/5537